795, AC

The
Concept of
FOLKLORE

The
Concept of
FOLKLORE

by Paulo de Carvalho-Neto

translated by

Jacques M. P. Wilson

University of Miami Press
Coral Gables, Florida

Translated from the second edition,
published under the title *Concepto de Folklore.*
Copyright © 1965 by The Macmillan Company

This translation copyright © 1971 by
University of Miami Press
Library of Congress Catalog Card Number 70–102693
ISBN 0–87024–166–4

Designed by Mary Lipson
Manufactured in the United States of America

Permissions to quote were generously granted by:
Alfred A. Knopf, Inc., for material from *How
Natives Think,* by Lucien Lévy-Bruhl; Prentice-Hall, Inc.,
for material from Alan Dundes, *The Study of
Folklore,* © 1965; The Macmillan Company for material
from *The Division of Labor in Society*
by Emile Durkheim, © 1949.

Contents

33234

To Celina and Cacilda,
my sisters

Foreword

The problems faced by Latin American folklore scholarship are in many ways quite familiar to folklorists in the United States. There is, for example, the same unevenness in distribution of workers in respect to the geographical areas where folklore may be found. Some important parts of Latin America abound in folklore materials; yet little serious collecting and much less scholarship has been done. Research has often been motivated by a kind of romantic nationalism similar to the regionalist enthusiasm that has motivated much folklore study in the United States and kept it at a rather uncomplicated level.

There are some interesting differences, however, in the general emphasis of folklore scholarship in Latin America and the United States. Usually monolingual, North American folklorists have looked principally to Great Britain for precedents in folklore studies. Latin American folklorists, on the other hand, have been influenced by the works of European masters in the field, as well as by Anglo-Americans. The result is a range of variation in the quality of scholarship even wider perhaps than in the United States. In some instances, what should have been important works are in reality naïve documents dedicated to romantic nationalist fervor. There is, however, an abundance of works of a theoretical and methodological sophistication that could well be emulated by folklorists in the United States.

It is to this latter group that the works of Paulo de Carvalho-Neto belong. Born in 1923 in Brazil, one of the countries in Latin America where scholarly interest in folklore has always been high, Carvalho early made his mark in his field of study. In 1949, just out of the University of Brazil, he became a cultural officer in the Brazilian diplomatic corps in Paraguay, where he proceeded to carry out the first systematic program of folklore research to be done in that country in addition to training Paraguayan scholars in the field. Still as professor, Carvalho passed from Paraguay to Uruguay in 1952, then, as cultural attaché to Ecuador in 1960, and finally in 1967 to Chile (from which country he came to the United States). Always his prime interest was to encourage folklore studies in his country of residence.

It was in Uruguay, in 1952, that Carvalho wrote his first folklore book, *Folklore del Paraguay,* based on field collections done by him and his students during 1949–1951. It is typical of Carvalho that this first book was not merely a collection of folklore but an essay at a systematic classification and analysis as well. But it was not until 1961, after some experiences that would have discouraged a less sanguine man than Carvalho-Neto, that *Folklore del Paraguay* saw print. Unalarmed by the troubles that beset *Folklore del Paraguay,* Carvalho continued his work in folklore studies, publishing in 1956 not one, but two works of a theoretical nature: *Concepto de folklore* and *Folklore y psicoanálisis.* These were followed in 1961 by the long-delayed *Folklore del Paraguay* and by a third theoretical work, *Folklore y educación.* Since that time, Carvalho's publications have been numerous, and it would take a good deal of space to even list them all.

It is to his first published work about folklore, *Concepto de folklore,* now appearing in English translation as *The Concept of Folklore,* that we now address ourselves. Characteristic of Carvalho-Neto and the tradition of folklore scholarship he represents, his first published work on folklore deals with theory instead of being a collection of folk songs as is so often the case in our own scholarly tradition. The Latin American folklorist usually takes less of an empirical view toward his subject than do most folklorists in the United States.

Because of this basic difference in point of view, some North American folklorists may find *The Concept of Folklore* too formalistic in style, with its well-structured development of themes and frequent references to the old masters. In the United States, people do not like to be "lectured to." When they lecture before their classes, North American professors seek to sound as though they are doing something else. They seek to avoid "didacticism," frequently falling back on phrases like "as all of us know" and "there is no necessity to dwell on the point" to generate the impression that their students know as much as they do. One of the sins of "didacticism" is the belaboring of the obvious. As we lean backward in our attempts to avoid this fault, we too often use terms without adequately defining them, and get into long and loud arguments with our colleagues that are based on misunderstandings of the way our words are used. In *The Concept of Folklore,* Paulo de Carvalho-Neto is not shy about being didactic, or about explaining his points in what some North Americans would consider an overly formal way. He does define his terms fully and adequately. The reader may not completely agree with all he says in the following pages, but he cannot say that Carvalho has not made his position clear.

But if we put Carvalho down as an old-fashioned formalist, we may be surprised to discover that back in 1956 he was already challenging such sacred terms as "oral tradition," not only because there is much folklore that is not transmitted by word of mouth (an obvious matter to Latin-American folklorists, who do not define folklore as oral literature), but because Carvalho questioned the term "tradition" itself, finding it "romantic and imprecise" (p. 34, 2nd Spanish edition; p. 142, 1st edition). Basing his argument more on logic and etymology than on the idea of folklore as process, he agrees with some of our younger folklorists in the United States today who would be happy to rid themselves of the term "oral tradition" once and for all.

Few North American folklorists today will fail to sympathize with Carvalho when he deplores the "chaos" of folklore theory (p. 95, Spanish edition), quoting a veteran folklorist who declared in São Paulo in 1954 that he had spent fifty years studying "something that no one knew exactly how to identify: folklore."

Carvalho-Neto's *Concepto de folklore* was not the first work on folklore theory to appear in Latin America. Nor does he stand alone among the original theorizers in folklore that the countries to the south of us have produced. But Carvalho in *Concepto de folklore* was a pioneer in his attempt to systematize his and others' ideas on folklore and to make them available to others. And it is perhaps as a teacher and systematizer that Paulo de Carvalho-Neto will be remembered best in years to come as one who has sought to enhance the frontiers of folklore scholarship in Latin America by spreading the word on an international scale. Heretofore, he has labored only among those who know Spanish or Portuguese. Now we can thank the University of Miami Press for introducing Carvalho-Neto to readers in the United States.

AMÉRICO PAREDES

Austin, Texas

Translator's Note

Only in recent years have scholars delved deeply into Folklore in an attempt to reach a comprehensive understanding of the traditions, beliefs, and values of a society. The fascinating and at times baffling study of "folk" practices has been a comparatively neglected area by North American scholars. While they have in recent years been described and analyzed by folklorists, ethnographers, and cultural anthropologists, few attempts have been made to synthesize the collected data into a theoretical framework covering Folklore, its nature, extent, and implications.

The Concept of Folklore by Brazil's leading Folklorist, Paulo de Carvalho-Neto, is a unique contribution. The author succinctly provides the reader with a sound theoretical basis for further readings and field research in this discipline. A prolific writer and researcher in South American folklore (Brazil, Uruguay, Paraguay, Ecuador, and Chile) as well as a dedicated teacher, it is only fitting that the University of Miami Press should make this work available to the English-speaking public as the first of several projected translations of his works.

Methodological problems involved in this translation were numerous. The author's classical Brazilian and Iberian pedagogical style makes extensive use of quotations and citations. References were inevitably made to appropriate Spanish translations of works written in French, German, or English. In order to make this translation a useful tool for American readers quotations and citations are taken from the latest English edition of the work or in the case of German and French works from authorized English translations.

Works falling in this category were:

Harry Alpert, *Emile Durkheim and his Sociology;* Harry E. Barnes and Howard Becker, *Social Thought from Lore to Science;* Ruth Benedict, *Race: Science and Politics;* Franz Boas, *Anthropology and Modern Life;* Juan Comas, *Racial Myths;* Emile Durkheim, *The Division of Labor in Society;* Emile Durkheim, *The Rules of Sociological Method;* Sigmund Freud, *An Outline of Psychoanalysis;* Sigmund Freud, "On Narcissism: An Introduction"; Sigmund Freud, *A General Introduction to Psychoanalysis;* Sigmund Freud, *The Interpretation of Dreams;* Sigmund Freud, *Totem and Taboo;* Sigmund Freud, *Three Essays on the Theory of Sexuality;* Edward Glover, *Freud or Jung;* Georg Hegel, *Philosophy of Mind;* Melville J. Herskovits, *Man and His Works: The Science of Cultural Anthropology;* Abram Kardiner, *The Individual and His Society; the Psychodynamics of Primitive Social Organization;* Lucien Lévy-Bruhl, *Primitive Mentality;* Lucien Lévy-Bruhl, *How Natives Think;* Robert H. Lowie, *The History of Ethnological Theory;* Bronislaw Malinowski, *A Scientific Theory of Culture and Other Essays;* C. K. Ogden and I. A. Richards, *The Meaning of Meaning;* A. R. Radcliffe-Brown, "On the Concept of Function in Social Science"; W. J. Thoms, "Folklore"; and Edward B. Tylor, *Primitive Culture.*

Some editorial reorganization that seemed appropriate in the American edition involved certain short chapters in the original work being consolidated and one unusually long chapter being subdivided. Thus Chapters 2 and 3 of the original appear in this edition as Chapter 2; Chapters 4 and 5 are combined into a new Chapter 3; Chapters 8, 9, and 10 into Chapter 9; and Chapters 11 and 12 into a new Chapter 10. The long Chapter 6 of the original is divided into new Chapters 4, 5, 6 and 8 in this edition. Finally, Chapter 17 of the original, a reference bibliography of Latin American manuals on General Folklore, appears as the Appendix to this edition.

J.M.P.W.

Introduction

Folklore, a branch of cultural anthropology, is the scientific study of the cultural acts of any people. These acts are characterized principally by being anonymous and noninstitutionalized, and eventually by being ancient, functional, and prelogical. The objective of Folklore is to discover the rules governing the formation, organization, and metamorphosis of these cultural acts for the benefit of mankind.

This is my theory, and I will try to explain it word by word.

For the purpose of this analysis, folklore is divided into two parts: one dealing with the folkloric act (folklore) and the other, the boundaries of folklore (Folklore). To differentiate between the science and the act, that is, between what is known about the folk and what the folk know, I have adopted the convention by which "folklore" with a lowercase letter refers to act, and "Folklore" with a capital refers to the science. When I have discussed other sciences, however, I have adhered to modern literary style, and have lowercased their initial letters.

In my definition the portion relating to boundaries of the science ends with the word "people," and the portion relating to the folklore act begins there. A further explanation is obviously required since every folkloric act is cultural but not every cultural activity is folkloric. The cultural state is a basic condition of the folklore act as are anonymity and noninstitutionalization. The remaining conditions of the definition are fortuitous.

Theories attempt in varying degrees to explain the fundamental questions concerning the matter under discussion. In our case, we will consolidate the concept of Folklore and folklore. Very frequently Folklore is better understood after having observed and analyzed folklore. This should be accomplished without falling into the exclusivist misconception of explaining a science only by the subject matter of the science.

Let us begin our complex inquiry and hope that the reader himself will reach the point of developing a group of fundamental theories that will help him cope with the vast and far-reaching boundaries of Folklore.

The
Concept of
FOLKLORE

1

On Being Cultural

PRINCIPAL CHARACTERISTICS OF A CULTURAL ACT

To discuss a cultural act or a social act is to talk about the same thing. Its principal characteristics were described by such classic authors as Francis Bacon (1561–1626), Auguste Comte (1798–1857), Émile Durkheim (1858–1917), and Karl Marx (1818–1883). Today no really serious students are not aware that its characteristics are: to be extrinsic, to be coercive, to be interdependent, and to be perfectionable.

To Be Extrinsic

The social act is performed beyond our individual conscience. Since it is an objective reality, it can well be appreciated how difficult it must have been for Durkheim to conceive a proposition that today seems so self-evident. His discussion of the characteristics of social acts is so definitive that I have here quoted extensively from it:

"Similarly, the church-member finds the beliefs and practices of his religious life ready-made at birth; their existence prior to his own implies their existence outside of himself. The system of signs I use to express my thought, the system of currency I employ to pay my debts, the instruments of credit I utilize in my commercial relations, the practices followed in my profession, etc., function independently of my own use of them. And these statements can be repeated for each member of society. Here, then, are ways of acting, thinking, and feeling that present the noteworthy property of existing outside the individual consciousness" (45).

To Be Coercive

The social act is coercive because it performs a coactive action on individual consciences. According to Durkheim's argument, these patterns of conduct or of thought are not only extrinsic to the individual, but in addition they are endowed with a coercive and imperative strength which imposes them regardless of our wishes.

> If I attempt to violate the law, it reacts against me so as to prevent my act before its accomplishment, or to nullify my violation by restoring the damage, if it is accomplished and reparable, or to make me expiate it if it cannot be compensated for otherwise. [. . .] In many cases the constraint is less violent, but nevertheless it always exists. If I do not submit to the conventions of society, if in my dress I do not conform to the customs observed in my country and in my class, the ridicule I provoke, the social isolation in which I am kept, produce, although in an attenuated form, the same effects as a punishment in the strict sense of the word. The constraint is nonetheless efficacious for being indirect. I am not obliged to speak French with my fellow-countrymen nor to use the legal currency, but I cannot possibly do otherwise. If I tried to escape this necessity, my attempt would fail miserably. As an industrialist, I am free to apply the technical methods of former centuries; but by doing so, I should invite certain ruin. Even when I free myself from these rules and violate them successfully, I am always compelled to struggle with them. When finally overcome, they make their constraining power sufficiently felt by the resistance they offer. The enterprises of all innovators, including successful ones, come up against resistance of this kind.
>
> Here, then, is a category of facts with very distinctive characteristics: it consists of ways of acting, thinking, and feeling, external to the individual, and endowed with a power of coercion, by reason of which they control him. These ways of thinking could not be confused with biological phenomena, since they consist of representations and of actions; nor with psychological phenomena, which exist only in the individual consciousness and through it. They constitute, thus, a new variety of phenomena; and it is to them exclusively that the term "social" ought to be applied (45).

Durkheim goes on to discuss the appropriateness of the terms he suggests. This is, of course, beside the point. What is important is to understand that our ideas and tendencies, for the most part, are not produced by us but rather they originate outside of ourselves, and that it is evident that they can only affect us as a result of having been imposed on us (45). At the present time, sociologists can establish the degree of coercibility of the acts. They are considered "folkways" when their violation is free from violent repression, and "mores" when they violation causes violent repression (92, pp. 433–436; 114).

To Be Interdependent

The social act is interdependent because at the same time it not only influences others but is also influenced by them. This is verified by the materialistic dialectic that explains it by the so-called "law of reciprocal action," according to which "everything exerts influence on everyone" (8, p. 120). Or, as Pascal poetically states, "Because a stone is cast into the sea, the entire sea is disturbed." Luiz de Aguiar Costa Pinto observes that it is for this reason, among others, "that society is an extremely complex reality." He finds, however, a degree of exaggeration in the dialectic law since it denies the logical principle of causality which distinguishes the fundamental reasons from the secondary and accessory ones (37).

The idea of interdependency of the cultural act is basic, especially for an understanding of cultural dynamics. To view the elements of the act and still not lose sight of the act is the aim of integral research.

To Be Perfectionable

The social act is perfectionable because it covers experiences as a result of its quality of being extrinsic to the individual. Man has progressed from caves to skyscrapers. This indicates our difference from the birds, bees, and ants. They are still the same. They are not characterized as having a culture since they are not cultural beings. Some experts believe they act as a reaction to their instincts or to their "embryonal cells." This means that they inherit their behavior at birth, while man must learn how to behave from the preceding generation (15).

THE CONCEPT OF CULTURE

Knowing now that the social or cultural act is primarily extrinsic, coercive, interdependent, and perfectionable, we need only agree on a definition encompassing the concept of culture. Among the many, we prefer that of Arthur Ramos, "It is the sum total of all human creations. . . . It is everything made or produced by man in either a material or nonmaterial sense" (98, p. 24). Here we do not, of course, refer to the common meaning of the term as implied in the phrase: "an individual is cultured," that is, he has many ideas, a great store of knowledge, or he is learned.

What Culture Is Not

Culture is not what at first glance it appears to be. It is neither race nor physical appearance. Man inherits it in a social manner (from society), and this process of transmission is not the same as racial or biological inheritance.

Culture *(Kultur)* and race are different ideational values. The idea of race is one "based on a classification of hereditary characteristics," while Ruth Benedict indicates that culture is the sociological name for learned behavior (15). To confuse these values is not merely an error or a primary demonstration of ignorance, it is racism, which today is a dangerous resource for political propaganda. This is the same racism that hoisted the banners of nazism-fascism in its attempt at world domination. Racism accepts the concept of superior or inferior races when the reality is that there are cultures that are more developed than others. The great material conquests of the German people were shallowly attributed to their physical qualities. But the protests of many scientists and other unbiased thinkers were soon heard against such misinformation. In December 1949, for example, experts brought together by UNESCO proclaimed a *Declaration on Race,* thundering against any ethnocentric affirmations. This outstanding declaration on the question of race and culture states textually that "all research conducted to determine if there exists any relationship between physical and mental characteristics have provided negative results" (118). According to genetic laws, then, man has the same capacity in all latitudes. He is not born into superior or inferior categories. Logically, racism had to fall, its hidden intentions revealed to all. It developed into a myth. After the symposium in Paris, Juan Comas, one of the participants, wrote a monograph on *The Racial Myths* (32). "Aggressive races" or "peaceful races" are also scientific falsehoods. They do not exist. What exists are cultures that are or are not agressive. Ruth Benedict, for example, cites the transition through the centuries of the Japanese from a peaceful to a warlike culture without any changes manifest in the race (15). Finally, we can conclude that old dictums "like father like son" or "a chip off the old block" are very relative. Children of Indians do not behave like Indians if, from their most tender age, they are raised in another culture.

In the field of Folklore the confusion of ideas reigning over race and culture produces laughable results. For some, seeing a Negro woman on the street brings the term "folklore" to mind. There are individuals who insist on seeing folklore in the color of one's skin or in the manner of combing one's hair.

Physical appearance, on the other hand, is individual, particular, and biotypological. There is one science which studies it, biotypology. It is different from culture, which is general and shared by the group and which is an aspect studied by culturology or ethnology, sociology, Folklore, and other cultural sciences. Incredible though it may seem, confusion still occurs. Even the "Pyknic type"* passes for folklore.

Cultural Act or Social Act

There has been no lack of studies refuting sociocultural synonymy. They accomplish their ends by fallacious arguments, and I will not follow them. A cultural act is the same as a social act. The only differences, and they are artificial ones, are of emphasis. The cultural act is more closely related to the property of man, the social one to the established practices of life in society. One is more closely related to anatomical studies and the other to physiological studies. In other words, the research methods and the manner of systematizing the data are always what separate the social sciences from each other. The limits separating them can only be clearly observed in practice. In 1954, at the International Congress of Folklore at São Paulo, Albert Marinus stated that the folkloric act is a social act, and I believe this is correct (79). But it would be more exact (and more conciliatory) to say the act is a sociocultural act.

---

*Pyknic type. Human type characterized by small stature, relatively short members, strong and rounded body forms. (E.g., Panza in Cervantes' *Don Quixote*.)

Culture and Civilization

I do not feel that there is any need to insist on the "cultural act" for the objectives that I have set out. But I do not want the word "civilization" to be used instead of "culture." Civilization is a historical and not an anthropological concept. The word comes from *civis,* city. The one who was civilized was a city dweller. This word acquired new emotional overtones to the degree that differences of habits between city dwellers and those in the countryside were identified. It became associated with the ideas of education, cleanliness, and good manners. In Greek, the same thing occurred with the word "polished." It no longer means the inhabitant of the *polis.* In contemporary times, "savage" no longer means an inhabitant of the forest *(selva).* Logically, then, a history of civilization is not a history of culture, but of the culture that has developed (97).

2

On Being Anonymous and Noninstitutionalized

ON BEING ANONYMOUS

From Cultural Anthropology to Folklore

Let us now proceed from the cultural act to the folkloric act. To do so new conditions must be added to the previously stated properties of the cultural act. Some of these conditions are specific or absolute characteristics while others are fortuitous, that is they may be included or not depending on the case. The specific conditions of the folkloric act that make it more than cultural are that it be anonymous and noninstitutionalized.

In other words, we now proceed from cultural anthropology to Folklore. The separation of the two sciences began in the second half of the past century. Remember that Folklore grew out of cultural anthropology. It is "that aspect of ethnology, etc., etc. . . ." described by Arthur Ramos (98, p. 25). Unfortunately, we do not know who dealt with the specific and fortuitous aspects first. If my memory does not fail me I have been the first to catalog them as such. They have been studied for a long time, however, and appear in the works of most modern scholars with an incredible amount of incoherency. The folkloric meaning of the word "anonymous" is the same as the vernacular meaning. As stated in the dictionary, "anonymous" is that which has no name or bears no author's name.

The Process of Anonymity

To understand the process of anonymity in folklore, we must clarify certain correlative aspects such as the following: the anonymous and the individual, anonymity and culture, creators and transmitters. It is axiomatic that no act because it is anonymous was created out of thin air. *Ex nihilo, nihil:* "Nothing is created out of nothingness; everything has its reason for being" (123). In other words, the idea of being anonymous does not exclude the individual. "It is logical to believe that everything had its own exclusive creator," says Luis Hoyos Sáinz (60, p. 38). Ismael Moya adds, "It is irrefutable that each work has someone responsible for its gestation" (84, p. 47). "All the works of a people . . . originate with the individual," writes Amadeu Amaral (6, p. 244). Augusto Raúl Cortazar adds, "Whether they be traditions transplanted from Spain, or the survival of indigenous ones from those who inhabited the region years ago, or recent transculturations, in every case each one had as its point of origin a primitive individual manifestation. This is particularly true when we deal with inventions or discoveries. A people, collectively and simultaneously, does not create cultural elements. These follow a trajectory beginning with the individual, and in some cases they finally include the group" (34, p. 239). Enrique de Gandía also states, "We do not believe that there are plebeian inspirations in music, poetry, or in any art at all. There was a time when democratic philosophies led scientists to state that a people created everything. Today we know that a people do not create anything; they only imitate. Everything that is beautiful and original is the work of one man alone, and he is a genius" (54, p. 121). If necessary it would be possible to cite additional authorities on this topic. The corollary is clear: in any given culture it is always possible, although in some cases hypothetically so, to discover the origin of actions that are considered anonymous.

Concurrently, a problem is inferred from this that can only be resolved by the correlation of culture and anonymity. Will the folkloric act lose its designation as such because, strictly speaking, it is no longer anonymous? No. Anonymity in folklore is not restricted to the act itself but is considered in relation to the culture where it exists. This means that if a society does not know the plebeian origins of its actions, thoughts, and emotions (even if the scholar does), they are virtually anonymous and may be folkloric. The following statement of Enrique de Gandía is consequently understandable, "A song whose author is known is not folkloric" (54, p.

157). Or the following from Moya, "Approximately ten percent of the population knows many sextains of the poem ('Martín Fierro'), not as authored by him (José Hernández, the author), but because they are heard in the course of time, and they do not suspect that they are Hernández's. Under such special conditions those passages of 'Martín Fierro' are folklore for those who recite them . . ." (84, p. 50).

Merely to research and discover how many members of a community do not know the author of an act does not necessarily define its condition as anonymous. *Verbi gratia*, popular art (sculptors, weavers, ceramists, and instrumentalists) because the plebeian artist always claims that he made the artifact. Undoubtedly, he is the creator. Is the article he produces anonymous? Much uncertainty assails the beginner in the science of Folklore in situations like this. The confusion disappears if anonymity refers to the author of the authors, the "creator." A means of avoiding more mistakes is to avoid confusing the term "creator" for "transmitter." The "transmitter" is an informant who frequently identifies himself as the "author." When the creator or author and the transmitter are the same person the act is not folkloric, although it can be if, potentially, it possesses the characteristics of a folkloric act. To this state of things is applied the qualifier *in statu nascendi*. It is, therefore, difficult to find genuine transmitters, because almost all transmitters are also creators. Because of his own personality, the transmitter tends to add to or modify those acts he acquires as his social heritage. In each piece of folklore there are, therefore, aspects which are not folkloric. It could be said, in summary, that the creator conceives the essence and form of the act, while the bearer transmits and modifies it.

The Indispensability of the Anonymous

These explanations of the anonymous aspect in folklore are not superfluous since it is one of its essential qualities. Among others, the following scholars recognize its need in the folkloric act: Rafael Jijena Sánchez and Bruno Jacovella (67, p. 20), Arnold Van Gennep (121, I, pp. 51–54), María Cadilla de Martínez (21, p. 45), Luis Hoyos Sáinz (60, p. 38), Félix Molina-Téllez (81, p. 38), Ismael Moya (84, p. 47), Alfredo Poviña (93, II, p. 656), and Efraín Morote Best (83, pp. 30–31).

ON BEING NONINSTITUTIONALIZED

A Pedagogical Theme

The folklorization of the anonymous cultural act is accomplished by its being transmitted by noninstitutionalized means. To explain this, we need to enter the field of the pedagogical sciences. We will see what is meant by transmission, and then by noninstitutionalized transmission. Before I begin that discussion, however, please note that I here talk about "noninstitutionalized transmission" and not "noninstitutionalized tradition." I believe the term "tradition" must be rejected and have spoken out against it since the first edition of my book.

The Transmission

The essential idea behind all process for the communication of knowledge is, first of all, learning. When we say that an "object" was transmitted, we mean that it was "learned." We can grasp the concept of learning if we break it down into its components: its phases, its characteristics, its objectives, and its causes. The "individual" and the culture are the elements of learning. Culture is "what is learned." Man is the individual or the person in the learning process, he "who learns." There is no transmission process without these two elements: culture and the individual.

The phases of learning are "integration," "psychological evolution," and "change of behavior." A thing is only learned when it is "integrated" by the individual. In this sense, learning is the integration of a legacy of experiences. It is evident that integration has taken place when the individual's behavior changes from what it was formerly, proving that the process of psychological evolution has taken place within him. Some theoreticians state, however, that, "not all behavioral changes result from learning," but rather from natural development, organic changes, or other causes. They cite the behavior of the drunken person as an example.

To avoid confusion between the terms "learning" and "forgetting," I shall identify characteristics and objectives of the learning process. In order to learn, the process must be continuous, progressive, and slow. This is observed daily in our children: they learn to suckle, to lisp, to walk; in sum, they learn to live. Naturally, they face a difficult struggle since they have to learn by themselves.

We cannot learn for our children, since no one learns for anyone else. We can, of course, show them how to learn, indicating to them ways of integrating culture. And most of the time we do this inadvertently by talking, playing, working, and so on.

The primary objective of learning is social accommodation, in other words, social balance, social adjustment. What causes this to happen? We know that changes in behavior occur because of "integration" and that the latter in turn results from "psychological evolution," but why does psychological evolution take place? The latter results from motivation. The motive of the action is what predisposes the individual to undergo psychological evolution. It comes from the Latin *motivus, a, um,* "that which moves, excites, or is effective in moving. *Movere, motare,* to move or to provide a motive" (24). Every action is consequently the result of a motive and tends to satisfy it. But for each satisfied motive new ones crop up that require new actions, which in turn require a new psychological evolution, new integration, and new behavior changes, in short, new learnings. In this sense, learning is considered an endless circular process.

For some time "impulse," "stimulus," and "need" were considered synonyms for motivation. According to Alfred Adler and other psychologists, there are different types of motivations: (1) Basic or fundamental motivations: hunger, thirst, fatigue, sleep, breathing, the vegetative functions in general. (2) Dominant motivations: the sense of community, love, work. And Thomas says that there are four basic desires: communication, security, importance, and new experiences (75).

In practice, it is important not to confuse motivation with the cultural deed. It is not culture by itself that creates psychological evolution in the individual, but, rather, the need to obtain it. Man does not learn to eat because food is placed before him, but because he is hungry. Food by itself does not represent need or motivation. It is hunger that motivates man to invent saucepans, dishes, and silverware. "It is said that man has *learned* when a type of behavior satisfies a need" (75).

Noninstitutionalized Transmission

There are two kinds of transmission. The idea of noninstitutionalized transmission can be understood by contrasting it with institutionalized transmission. In institutionalized transmission or teaching, learnings are organized, directed, and arrayed in graduated degrees of difficulty. In noninstitutionalized transmission, they are neither organized, directed, nor organized in graduated degrees of difficulty. Folklore takes the latter direction in that it is neither official, academic, nor aristocratic.

Synonyms of Noninstitutionalized Transmission

I am responsible for the use of the term "noninstitutionalized" in our field. I adapted it from the field of education. I think the term an excellent one and, especially, because it is used in that neighboring discipline. As a result, I reject the terms "oral transmission" and "spontaneity." "Oral" is an inadequate term for folklore. It refers to the verbal, the vocal, and is related to the mouth. We know very well that among folklore acts some that appeal to the senses cannot be transmitted orally alone, but require, in addition, the visual dimension. These include payés,* dances, embroidery, transportation, and architecture. In short, magic, social, and ergological folklore cannot be transmitted solely by oral means. These acts are learned through "motor-perception" while others (poetic narrative, and linguistic folklore) are learned through "ideation" and "verbalization," terms borrowed from educational psychology. There was a time when the term "oral" was widely accepted. "Oral Literature" became almost synonymous with Folklore. Indeed, in 1877, Gaston Paris suggested the use of the term oui-dire. This term emphasizes the oral aspect of Folklore. "Oui-dire"** was to be the science and "ouidiristes" its adherents (98, p. 14).

Transmission and Tradition

When involved with folklore, the term "tradition" must be rejected. I have spoken out against it since the first edition of my book. I stated: "This new proposal will have the advantage of absolutely eliminating the use of the term tradition which has been responsible for so much confusion. We can completely eliminate its use. And what is more, we feel it is a lay term, applied to folklore during the initial prescientific work in our discipline. It is one of the many romantic stereotypes that we run up against, that is to say,

*Payés: a term used by the Paraguayan people to identify magic.
**Oui-dire: "to hear tell."

ideas created, and experiences fixed by habit. When *traditional condition* was referred to in this study, it is only an attempt to not turn our backs completely on an almost universally adopted rule."*

Let us then limit tradition to its literal meaning, to the central idea of transmission. Undoubtedly in the future we will eliminate it from our scientific vocabulary. In fact, the term "tradition" is dangerous for our purposes since folklore does not accept it etymologically, but rather in its conventional figurative sense, which permits subjective interpretations.

Etymologically, "tradition" is "transmission" but not all "transmission" is "tradition." José Imbelloni states: "Let us remember that this word is the abstract imperative of the verb *tradere*; derived from it and with similar endings are formed sister words: *translation, betrayal,*** and *traction*, which, with subtle semantic differences, mean: the translation of one language to another, surrender to the enemy, and the act of physically conveying a heavy body. It is then inferred that *tradition* does not properly indicate an object, but rather the act of its transfer. Consequently, in our discipline [Folklore] *tradition* identifies the mechanism through which we inherit the treasures of our forefathers" (62, p. 59). Antonio de Valbuena states that tradition is "ancient knowledge or opinion, derived from one person or another. *Traditio, onis; rei à majoribus ad posteros translatio; nudi verbi testimonio acepta res*" (119). Manuel do Canto and Castro Mascarenhas Valdez also state that tradition is "information about an act, transmitted by parents to their children, from generation to generation. *Traditio, onis.* Oral tradition: that which is transmitted by word of mouth" (24). Other lexicographers state the same thing.

The word "tradition," then, is not appropriate, primarily because of its metaphoric implication. Metaphorically, it embraces the idea of transmission and the idea of being noninstitutionalized, anonymous, and ancient. But we will always have to conceptualize "tradition" through ideas suggested by other words. Why then not handle the ideas through appropriate terminology, rather than defining them by words having multiple connotations?

---

*First edition of *Concepto de Folklore*. Montevideo, Livraria Monteiro Lobato, 1956, 191 pp. See p. 142. In the second edition, p. 34.
**Translator's Note: In Spanish—"traición."

3

On Being Ancient and On Being Functional

ON BEING ANCIENT

Etymology of "Ancient"

Etymologically, "ancient" is the adjective of "antiquity," that is to say, that possessed of antiquity. *Antiquus, a, um:* veteran. To the *old,* according to custom and usage, ancient. *Veteres, prisci sapientes:* ancient, old, very ancient, advanced in years. "Antiquity," on the other hand, comes from *Antiquitas, atis. Veterum sapientia, vel sapientes antiquitate commendabilis:* antiquity: precedence in time for the performance of a task; plural: antiquities (119, p. 24).

The Measure of Folkloric Antiquity

The measure of folkloric antiquity is the largest problem in this discussion. A table of reference, a measure of time, or a concrete criterion has not yet been devised to measure it. We say that it is more or less ancient, or not very old, and this is a subjective judgment that is incompatible with the scientific categorization of Folklore. This is particularly true when we consider that allied disciplines such as geology, history, paleontology, and archeology even have chemical processes to determine the age of specimens, in addition to a chronological organization for their classification. Dealing with this question, Arnold Van Gennep wrote a special chapter on "The Relative Age of Legends," in which he states, "the relative age of tales, legends, and myths was one of the most discussed problems of the nineteenth century" (120, p. 29). According to Enrique de Gandía, "the chronological limits of tradition cannot be determined in a fixed and exact manner. The present is not tradition because it is not old. However, things that are half a century old in a country that has only four centuries of continental historical existence can begin to be considered as a tradition and as folklore" (54, p. 162). Very well, half a century? Why fifty years in relation to four hundred and fifty years? José Imbelloni also studied this matter in essays entitled "Concerning a timeless past" and "Distant substrata and recent substrata." He states, "Folklore's objective is to capture not only the relics belonging to a distant substratum, according to the studies of the Tylor and Lubbock period, but also those which belong to the more recent periods including those which have just preceded us" (62, pp. 74–75). We still have the same problem. What does this mean in figures? How many years separate the period which immediately precedes us from the present time?

The Survivals

Finally, ancient events are generally referred to as "survivals," from the Latin *supervivere, superstitem esse*. The action or effect of survival, living longer than others, living after another person has died (24). Edward B. Tylor first proposed the term's use in discussing folklore and today the use of "folkloric survival" is common. Tylor begins his interpretation by stating:

> These are processes, customs, opinions, and so forth, which have been carried on by force of habit into a new state of society different from that in which they had their original home, and they thus remain as proofs and examples of an older condition of culture out of which a newer has been evolved. Thus, I know an old Somerset-shire woman whose hand-loom dates from the time before the introduction of the "flying shuttle," which new-fangled appliance she has never even learnt to use, and I have seen her throw her shuttle from hand to hand in true classic fashion; this old woman is not a century behind her times, but she is a case of survival. Such examples often lead us back to the habits of hundreds and even thousands of years ago. The ordeal of the Key and Bible, still in use, is a survival; the Midsummer bonfire is a survival; the Breton peasants' All Souls' supper for the spirits of the dead is a survival. The simple keeping up of ancient habits is only one part of the transition from old into new and changing times. The serious business of ancient society may be seen to sink into the sport of later generations, and its serious belief to linger on in nursery folk-lore, while superseded habits

of old-world life may be modified into new-world forms still powerful for good and evil (117, p. 16).

Naturally, before selecting this term, Tylor had doubts. He had
almost decided on "superstition" instead of "survival" since these
terms mean literally more or less the same thing. He did not do so
only because of the semantic evolution of the first word which has
come to include a pejorative meaning. He wrote,

> Such a proceeding as this would be usually, and not improperly,
> described as a superstition; and, indeed, this name would be given
> to a large proportion of survivals generally. The very word "super-
> stition," in what is perhaps its original sense of a "standing over"
> from old times, itself expresses the notion of survival. But the term
> superstition now implies a reproach, and though this reproach may
> be often cast deservedly on fragments of a dead lower culture em-
> bedded in a living higher one, yet in many cases it would be harsh,
> an even untrue. For the ethnographer's purpose, at any rate, it is
> desirable to introduce such a term as "survival," simply to denote
> the historical fact which the word "superstition" is now spoiled for
> expressing (117, I, pp. 71–72).

Using this criteria Tylor came to write a chapter on "survival in
civilization" in which he deals with such survivals as children's
games, traditional sayings, proverbs, and magical practices.

In time, the English school of anthropology—Andrew Lang,
James George Frazer, and others as well as Tylor—developed further the idea of survival in Folklore (98, pp. 123–124). At the same
time, Paul Sébillot introduced it in France (121, p. 96). Now, this
idea has become fundamental. Luis Hoyos Sáinz (60, pp. 33–35)
and Julio Caro Baroja (26, p. 23) discussed it in Spain, José Imbelloni (62, p. 58), Carlos Vega (122, pp. 23–29) and Alfredo
Poviña (93, p. 657) in Argentina, and Arthur Ramos (101, pp.
326–333; 98, p. 123), Édison Carneiro (25, p. 11) and Amadeu
Amaral (6) in Brazil, to name but a few.

The Nonancient Folkloric Act

For many decades antiquity was a *sine qua non* condition of the
folklore act. This term even became synonymous with, and also included, the science of Folklore. William John Thoms stated in a
letter: "Your words frequently show your interest for what we in

England call Popular Antiquities or Popular Literature" (116). The Brazilian Congress on Folklore of 1951, however, supported the claims of some scholars as to the viable existence of folkloric acts without the aspect of "antiquity," that is, new folklore acts *in statu nascendi,* and since then the essentiality of this item is questioned. The charter of the Brazilian Folklore Congress states, "The observations conducted on contemporary folklore without the traditional foundation are also considered proper" (61). In other words, these lack the basis of antiquity.

ON BEING FUNCTIONAL

The Concept of Function

"Functional" is a derivative of the verb "to function," *functio, onis, ar,* to perform a function. In the social sciences, culture performs a function in order to satisfy its motivation. We already know what motivation is, and we discussed it as a psycho-pedagogical concept. The concept of function, on the other hand, is fundamentally ethnological. We cited the example of hunger. As a result of its action, man creates features that facilitate his procurement of food. Function, then, is the objective that justifies the existence of culture. What are spoons used for? To what motivation do they respond?

Function and "Cultural Change"

It will be understood that cultural changes result from their function. Culture undergoes continuous transformation in order to better discharge its functions, to serve better, to satisfy in a better way. The motivations and functions, nevertheless, are inalterable factors from generation to generation. What changes is the culture, because it is dynamic *par excellence.* Something is widely accepted because it "works," it functions best. I say "accepted" rather than "attained" because not everyone can acquire what is most recommended.

Folklore: Nascent, Living, Dying, and Dead

It is during the process of cultural change that sequences of cultural values with identical functions are created. Those most recently developed are generally the most functional. The others survive until they disappear. Their final redoubt is in the recollections of old people. Based on time and function, the following categories of events can be pointed out: events *in statu nascendi,* live events, events *moribundus,* and dead events. *Mutatis mutandis,* there is folklore in the process of growth, living folklore, folklore in the process of dying out, and dead folklore.

Folklore in the process of dying out is perpetuated by a few individuals in the community and has almost lost its function. It is sheltered in people's memories and only comes to life in conversations dealing with the past. Dead folklore axiomatically is that which no longer exists even in the memory of the old people. Information about it is contained in old documents such as expedition records and archives. Living folklore is that which exists at the present time.

These considerations remind me of Yuri M. Sokolov when he says that "folklore is the echo of the past, but at the same time it is the powerful voice of the present" (25, p. 29). Bruno Jacovella also states that "There is a current or living folklore, which is folklore, and a historical or dead folklore which *was* folklore" (67, p. 27). Furthermore, "products of folklore are found in two states: a) functionally, full of vigor, intertwined with each other, serving a social group, and integrated in its life; b) virtually decrepit and isolated, surviving only in the mechanical or affective memory of some individuals who are generally mature, if not senile" (64, p. 7).

Definitions of Function

Let us now examine the classical definitions of function and functionalism. According to Alfred Reginald Radcliffe-Brown, function is the contribution made by part of an activity to the entire activity of which it is a part (94). In his article, "On The Concept of Function in the Social Sciences," the English scholar develops the idea of "social structure" and superimposes on it the idea of "function." "Structure" can be studied from three points of view: its social morphology, its social physiology, and its development. He sees the search for "function" as primarily a study of social physiology; and, as an example, he states that the *function* of a recurring activity like the punishment of a criminal or a funeral ceremony is the role that it plays in social life as an entity and, at the same time, the contribution it performs in maintaining structural continuity.

Bronislaw Malinowski (1884–1942), the originator of the functional school of culture, discusses and documents his disquisitions, principally in *A Scientific Theory of Culture and Other Essays.* This work should be mandatory reading on this topic. For the analysis of a group, he separates "constituent norms" from "function." According to the Polish scholar, constituent norms represent the idea of "institution," as it is conceived by its members and defined by the community. Function, on the other hand, is the role which the very institution plays in the total scheme of culture (77). It must be emphasized that in functionalism, institution is any fixed model of thought or conduct upheld by a group of individuals (that is, by a society) that can be communicated, that enjoys general acceptance, and whose violation or change produces a certain disquiet in the individual or the group (69; also 77). "For function can not be defined in any other way than the satisfaction of a need by an activity in which human beings cooperate, use artifacts, and consume goods" (77, p. 39). Huntington Cairns clearly perceived this point of Malinowski's. He stated that Malinowski "was convinced that cultural phenomena were not the consequence of capricious inventiveness or simple borrowing, but were determined by basic needs and the possibilities of satisfying them" (77, vi-vii). For our part, we have verified that Malinowski conceived the same circular process of learning in ethnology that is so dear to educational psychology. He stated that from the point of view of functional analysis, no real revolution or invention, no social or intellectual change, ever takes place without new needs having been fulfilled (77).

Durkheim, Precursor of Functionalism

Although Malinowski and Radcliffe-Brown were those who organized functionalism into a school, the possibility of adapting "functionalism" to social studies has been attempted since Durkheim. According to Radcliffe-Brown, Émile Durkheim was the first to apply functionalism to a strictly scientific study of society (94). In fact, Durkheim (1858–1917) sketches out the problem in his *Les Règles de la Méthode Sociologique* of 1895. Expanding upon the findings of Radcliffe-Brown, I must note that two years prior to *Les Règles,* Durkheim had begun to draft this idea in his

The Division of Labor in Society. Here the passage on the meaning of the word "function" is fundamental to this study and is the point from which he continued later. The concept of function is transcendental for Durkheim, and because of this we are amazed that the modern functionalists scarcely recognize the French scholar as their *precursor emeritus.*

With the explicit intention of reinstating Durkheim as the originator of the concept of functionalism I will cite his passage in its entirety.

> The word *function* is used in two quite different senses. Sometimes it suggests a system of vital movements, without reference to their consequences; at others it expresses the relation existing between these movements and corresponding needs of the organism. Thus, we speak of the function of digestion, of respiration, etc.; but we also say that digestion has as its function the incorporation into the organism of liquid or solid substances designed to replenish its losses, that respiration has for its function the introduction of necessary gases into the tissues of an animal for the sustainment of life, etc. It is in the second sense that we shall use the term. To ask what the function of the division of labor is, is to seek for the need which it supplies. When we have answered this question, we shall be able to see if this need is of the same sort as those to which other rules of conduct respond whose moral character is agreed upon.
>
> We have chosen this term because any other would be inexact or equivocal. We cannot employ *aim* or *object* and speak of the end of the division of labor exists *in the light of results* which we are going to determine. The terms, "results" or "effects," would be no more satisfactory, because they imply no idea of correspondence. On the other hand, the term "role," or "function," has the great advantage of implying this idea, without prejudging the question as to how this correspondence is established, whether it results from an intentional and preconceived adaptation or an aftermath adjustment. What is important for our purposes is to establish its existence and the elements of its existence; not to inquire whether there has been a prior presentiment of it, nor even if it has been sensibly felt afterward (44, pp. 49–50).

In *Les Règles,* Durkheim establishes the difference between "function" and "effective cause." When one undertakes the task of explaining a social phenomenon, the effective cause that produces it must be separated from the function that it fulfills.

Importance of the Concept of Function

It is function that binds culture to man, and its importance must not be underestimated. Man in a given area under study will not be understood by simple cultural-anatomical records. The precariousness of human relations stems from this in many cases, since mutual respect arises only from the mutual knowledge resulting from the study of function.

4

On Being Prelogical—
Edward B. Tylor

The term "prelogical" was first introduced to the social sciences by Lévy-Bruhl. Technically speaking, it refers to an act in which the "causality relation" is infantile; that is, the act is motivated by individual feeling rather than by scientific reasoning. In psychological phraseology, the prelogical act is autistic, prompted by the libido in its primitive stages of development.

The concept of an event functioning with basic forms contrary to Aristotelian logic has been developed by many scholars. Tylor named the ascientific mentality "animistic," Ribot named it "affective," and Lévy-Bruhl chose to call it "prelogical." Later we find Freud's term, "narcissistic."

Before we commence our review of the contributions of Tylor, Théodule Ribot, Lucien Lévy-Bruhl, and Sigmund Freud, I think it is interesting to note, parenthetically, the influence of Ribot, a psychologist, on the thinking of Tylor, an ethnologist. These disciplines, ethnology and psychology, do collaborate, with the result that in our time we see books on the psychology of Folklore and the coining of a new label, "cultural psychologist."

The specific observations of Tylor that contributed to Lévy-Bruhl's concept of the prelogical are: evolutionism, convergence, animism, and the primitive relationship of causality. They are dealt with primarily in *Researches into the Early History of Mankind and the Development of Civilization,* published in 1865, and *Primitive Culture: Researches into the Development of Mythology, Philosophy, Religion, Language, Art, and Custom,* published in 1871. Note that all of Tylor's theses on primitive mentality were criticized by Lévy-Bruhl; and, in the main, with Ribot's concurrence. When these ideas were expressed by Tylor, Ribot's *Logique des Sentiments*, published in 1905, had not yet appeared.

TYLOR'S THEORIES

Evolutionism

Herbert Spencer (1820–1903) developed the theory of evolutionism. Tylor assimilated perfectly the belief that the development of civilization is controlled by the so-called *laws of evolution*. Based on them, he conceived a plan for social development which included "savage," "barbarous," and "civilized" societies. He also developed his famous "theory of degeneration" which seems to be a rather outdated precursor of what is now referred to as the "theory of acculturation." Such ideas presupposed a scale of values, in other words, the classification of inferior and superior beings in the human species. "Primitive," for example, became a word loaded with prejudice that always invokes the idea of inferiority.

Note Franz Boas' definition: "Primitive people are those whose activities are but little diversified, whose forms of life are simple and uniform, and whose culture in its form and content is poor and intellectually inconsequential" (16). To avoid prejudice, we now conceptualize "primitive" as those elements that are "pregraphemic." Concerning this matter, consult Octávio da Costa Eduardo (36).

It is unfortunate that in assigning superior and inferior qualities to the different peoples of the earth, evolutionism used a comparative criterion, one based hierarchically downward from the culture of those who are doing the classifying. The balance of the cultures were aligned in descending order until reaching the barbarians, the savages. Today, this error in judgment is known by the term "ethnocentricism," or "cultural ethnocentricism." Donald Pierson writes:

Ethnocentricism is the tendency to see the world and what goes on in it through the colored glasses of the primary group, which places it in the center of everything. Thus their own customs are felt to be natural, true, and superior and the different customs of the other groups are judged to be quaint, peculiar, abnormal, mistaken, unintelligible, absurd, and even offensive and repugnant. Thus the behavior of *our group* is the *norm* used to evaluate that of any other group. Its function is to strengthen their customs and the control they exercise over the individual (92, p. 432).

According to Freud, the aborigines of Australia became the "most savage, backward, and miserable" tribes in existence, and it was these observations that gave him material for his studies on totem and taboo (52). Basing his judgments on Robert Southey, Tylor believed that the gauchos of Uruguay for their part would be on middle ground, having a detestable, brutal life without any comforts, degenerate but not savage. He tells of the gauchos of the Pampas of South America, a race of horse herders, mestizos of Europeans and Indians who are pictured seated on the skulls of oxen, preparing soup in the horns of these same animals, which are buried in hot ashes, and eating meat without vegetables.

The mestizos of gauchos and savages would be savages, continues Tylor, and one more step would enable civilized individuals to be absorbed by savage tribes and adopt their life, and yet not change it. The children of these once-civilized individuals would still be savages (117). Examples of "savages" are numerous in Tylor's works. The observations of Issaurat (one of his biographers) are to the point, "What one notes above all is the abundance of documents. One finds them by piles, by heaps, by mountains, and when these are cleared there are still others" (76, p. 83).

Lévy-Bruhl then disagreed with Tylor's evolutionism. Because it was ethnocentric, it was subjective or nonscientific, with prior answers for everything. He accused him of stifling the advance of the English school and of not getting greater benefit from the comparative method. In spite of this, Lévy-Bruhl was also charged with being an evolutionist by the historical-culturalists (101, p. 283). According to Richard Thurnwald, the culturalists were also in part evolutionists; the influence of Tylorian evolutionism was that strong (104, p. 418).

Last but not least, it is worth adding that many of evolutionism's roots have ramifications in contemporary racism. In fact, according to F. H. Hankins, Spencer postulates the existence of an intimate correlation between the state of cultural advancement and their intellectual levels and their inherent character, this being his gravest mistake (13, I). Spencer's error is a common one. Any evolutionist study contains expressions such as "inferior race" and "superior race." *Verbi gratia* even the work of our great Raymundo Nina Rodrigues, whose affection for Tylor was criticized and corrected more than once by Arthur Ramos, his own disciple.

Convergence

In addition to explaining the "progress" of culture by evolutionism, Tylor tried to explain the obscure problem of its origin; and to do so he developed the theory of "convergence," also called "independent development," "parallelism," or "recurrence." He aligned himself against the "diffusionists" or "historical-culturalists" or even "geographic historians." The latter were cultural monogenists, that is, those who upheld the hypothesis of a single origin for each cultural trait.

The diffusionists believed that the traits had been spreading from a single source in space and time. They went to Friedrich Ratzel to discover this idea of spatial cultural migration (98, p. 93), hence the appropriateness of the term "diffusionism." Upon extending geographic diffusion to time, the term "historical" was adopted. In historical-culturalism or diffusionism, the scholars retrogress from one culture to another, and compare them in order to reach the first, or supposedly the first, culture. In this research process, they created cultural *stracta (Kulturshichten)*. For this reason, Thurnwald, as we have stated, censured them for being essentially evolutionists (104, p. 418). Adolph Graebner, Willy Foy, B. Ankermann, Wilhelm Schmidt, and, in America, Imbelloni, among others, are historical-culturalists. Like so many ideas, diffusionism was subject to exaggeration, and the result was the so-called hyper-diffusionism that is found primarily in the work of Elliot Smith and his group of Egyptologists for whom Egypt was the cradle of universal culture.

The parallelists, as opposed to the diffusionists, are cultural polygenists. They established the origin of events "in various parts of the earth when the same causes and conditions were present." In other words, *quod semper, quod ubique, quod ab omnibus,* that is, always, everywhere, and for everyone (98, p. 121; 101, p. 280; 104, p. 288). As a historical complement, we must add that Tylor began with the theory of "fundamental ideas" *(Elementar gedanken)* of Adolf Bastian (1826–1905). Tylor acknowledges his debt to Bastian in the preface of the first edition of his *Primitive Culture.* Arthur Ramos correctly observed that "Bastian did not deny the possibility of the diffusion of cultural traits from one province to another. But this was secondary and complementary. The essential was the law of psychic unity expressed in the concept of *fundamental ideas* which would almost always be expressed practically as *ideas of the people (Volkergendanken)"* (98, p. 123).

It was on this point, specifically, that Lévy-Bruhl attacked Tylorian "convergence." He finds that those defending the previously cited Latin aphorism do so because they admit that the savage and civilized mentalities are identical to each other. In other words, the analogy of cultural traits explained by "independent development" presupposes a sameness of the human spirit, an absence of qualitative differences between savage and civilized reasoning, a common mental state, a universal logic. What Lévy-Bruhl did not specifically find in Tylor was the beneficent influence of Ribot's thinking. At the outset, Tylor did not take advantage of the existence of two logics, perceptual and formal. Tylor's "primitives" would think with the formal traditional Aristotelian logic of the "adult, civilized, white man."

They took it for granted that the facts could be explained *in one way only.* Do the collective representations of the communities in question arise out of higher mental functions identical with our own, or must they be referred to a mentality which differs from ours to an extent yet to be determined? Such an alternative as the latter did not occur to their minds (72).

Continuing, Lévy-Bruhl clarifies that the identity of a human mind at all times and in all places is accepted by the English school as a postulate, or better yet, as an axiom.

There is no need to demonstrate it, or even formally enunciate it: it is an understood principle, and too evident for any consideration of it to be necessary (72).

Tylor, subjected to this axiom, tried to explain primitive mentalities by the processes and habits of civilized mentalities. Lévy-Bruhl's criticism of Tylor's theory of convergence is as cruel as that leveled against the evolutionist theory of the same author. In spite of this, they both allied themselves against diffusionism. It could be said concerning this that Lévy-Bruhl is a more advanced parallelist.

What is the present state of the diffusionist and parallelist theories? Diffusionism for Arthur Ramos now belongs to the history of folklore: "... it includes outdated data and hypothesis, but it still has certain interesting points that are not completely worthless. Thus, if we limit ourselves to a single narrow belief about a place or initial point of origin—in India, in Egypt . . . such theses are controversial. However, if we consider a probable place for initial dissemination, to follow the latter transformations by diffusion, we will realize very extensive results" (98, p. 93). The diffusionists' ideas concerning a cultural cycle or cultural *stracta* were totally rejected, since North Americans preferred to introduce the idea of "cultural area" free from evolutionist connotations. The validity of historical-culturalism in our day, once the mistakes we have pointed out have been corrected, is evident, even for Folklore. Luís da Câmara Cascudo is an authentic, modern, historical-culturalist. He tries to answer the *how* of folkloric culture, while Ramos, for example, tries to answer the *why*. Ramos is a functionalist who tries to capture the personality of culture. He also mastered the psychoanalytical methodology of Folklore, whose fundamentals were developed by Freud in his monumental *Interpretation of Dreams* (51), a work that we shall analyze in chapter VII.

Parallelism should not be completely censured either. In a certain way, it comes close to the modern psychological theories of culture that ascribe the stimulus for human creativity to "necessity," to "motivation." In synthesis, both theories, diffusionism and parallelism, in spite of their evident flaws, prepared for the advance of anthropological studies in our time. As Ramos points out, anthropological studies leave research into the origin of cultural traits to one side and concentrate with greater benefit on their nature (98, p. 35). He adds that the problem of the origin of cultural traits "is considered today difficult if not impossible to solve. It belongs to that series of ethnological investigations of the past century which were concerned with investigating the origin of institutions through endless extensive theoretical discussions" (98, p. 92).

Animism

In addition to convergence, the identity of logic as it was axiomatically structured by Tylor and his English school contributed also to the conceptual development of animism. Without admitting the existence of two logics, that is, knowing beforehand that this intellect is the same among the primitives and us, all that was left to verify is how mental functions identical to ours could produce these representations and relationships" (72). Tylor was amazed by the collective representations of the primitives that were alien to our representations, and he had recourse for this to the idea of the existence of a quantitative difference of logic. There was no difference, whatsoever, in primitive and civilized reasoning, no qualitative difference, that is, two logics; but, nevertheless, there did exist a quantitative difference. Lévy-Bruhl indicates that the concept of animism appeared at this point in Tylor's work. And he concludes that the animist hypothesis is an immediate consequence of the axiom that dominated the studies of the English school of anthropology (72). In order to document this statement more fully, let us read the principles of animism expounded by Tylor himself in the following selected passages:

> Animism takes in several doctrines which so forcibly conduce to personification, that savages and barbarians, apparently without an effort, can give consistent individual life to phenomena that our utmost stretch of fancy only avails to personify in conscious metaphor. An idea of pervading life and will in nature far outside modern limits, a belief in personal souls animating even what we call inanimate bodies, a theory of transmigration of souls as well in life as after death, a sense of crowds of spiritual beings sometimes flitting through the air, but sometimes also inhabiting trees and rocks and waterfalls, and so lending their own personality to such material objects—all these thoughts work in mythology with such manifold coincidence, as to make it hard indeed to unravel their separate action.
>
> Such animistic origin of nature-myths shows out very clearly in the great cosmic group of Sun, Moon, and Stars. In early philosophy throughout the world, the Sun and Moon are alive and as it were human in their nature. Usually contrasted as male and female, they nevertheless differ in the sex assigned to each, as well as in their relations to one another. Among the Mbocobis of South America, the Moon is a man and the Sun his wife, and the story is told how she once fell down and an Indian put her up again, but she fell a second time and set the forest blazing in a deluge of fire (117, I, pp. 287–288). . . . To the theory of Animism belong those endless tales which all nations tell of the presiding genii of nature, the

spirits of cliffs, wells, waterfalls, volcanos, the elves and wood nymphs seen at times by human eyes when wandering by moonlight or assembled at their fairy festivals. Such beings may personify the natural objects they belong to, as when, in a North American tale, the guardian spirit of waterfalls rushes through the lodge as a raging current, bearing rocks and trees along in its tremendous course, and then the guardian spirit of the islands of Lake Superior enters in the guise of rolling waves covered with silver-sparkling foam (117, pp. 294–295).

. . . I prepose here, under the name of Animism to investigate the deep-lying doctrine of Spiritual Beings, which embodies the very essence of Spiritualistic as opposed to Materialistic philosophy. Animism is not a new technical term, though now seldom used. From its special relation to the doctrine of the soul, it will be seen to have a peculiar appropriateness to the view here taken of the mode in which theological ideas have been developed among mankind. The word Spiritualism, though it may be, and sometimes is, used in a general sense, has this obvious defect to us, that it has become the designation of a particular modern sect, who indeed hold extreme spiritualistic views, but cannot be taken as typical representatives of these views in the world at large. The sense of Spiritualism in its wider acceptation, the general belief in spiritual beings, is here given to Animism.

Animism characterizes tribes very low in the scale of humanity, and thence ascends, deeply modified in its transmission, but from first to last preserving an unbroken continuity, into the midst of high modern culture. Doctrines adverse to it, so largely held by individuals or schools, are usually due not to early lowness of civilization, but to later changes in the intellectual course, to divergence from, or rejection of, ancestral faiths; and such newer developments do not affect the present enquiry as to the fundamental religious condition of mankind. Animism is, in fact, the groundwork of the Philosophy of Religion, from that of savages up to that of civilized men. And although it may at first sight seem to afford but a bare and meagre definition of a minimum of religion, it will be found practically sufficient; for where the root is, the branches will generally be produced. It is habitually found that the theory of Animism divides into two great dogmas, forming parts of one consistent doctrine; first, concerning souls of individual creatures, capable of continued existence after the death or destruction of the body; second, concerning other spirits, upward to the rank of powerful deities. Spiritual beings are held to affect or control the events of the material world, and man's life here and hereafter; and it being considered that they hold intercourse with men, and receive pleasure or displeasure from human actions, the belief in their existence leads naturally, and it might almost be said inevitably, sooner or later to active reverence and propitiation. Thus Animism, in its full development, includes the belief in souls and in a future state, in controlling deities and subordinate spirits, these doctrines practically resulting in some kind of active worship (117, I, pp. 425–427).

. . . The first branch of the subject to be considered is the doctrine of human and other Souls, an examination of which will occupy the rest of the present chapter. What the doctrine of the soul is among the lower races, may be explained in stating the present theory of its development. It seems as though thinking men, as yet at a low level of culture, were deeply impressed by two groups of biological problems. In the first place, what is it that makes the difference between a living body and a dead one; what causes waking, sleep, trance, disease, death? In the second place, what are those human shapes which appear in dreams and visions? Looking at these two groups of phenomena, the ancient savage philosophers probably made their first step by the obvious inference that every man has two things belonging to him, namely, a life and a phantom. These two are evidently in close connexion with the body, the life as enabling it to feel and think and act, the phantom as being its image or second self; both, also, are perceived to be things separable from the body, the life as able to go away and leave it insensible or dead, the phantom as appearing to people at a distance from it. The second step would seem also easy for savages to make, seeing how extremely difficult civilized men have found it to unmake. It is merely to combine the life and the phantom. As both belong to the body, why should they not also belong to one another, and be manifestations of one and the same soul? Let them then be considered as united, and the result is that well-known conception which may be described as an apparitional-soul, a ghost-soul. This, at any rate, corresponds with the actual conception of the personal soul or spirit among the lower races, which may be defined as follows: It is a thin unsubstantial human image, in its nature a sort of vapour, film, or shadow; the cause of life and thought in the individual it animates; independently possessing the personal consciousness and volition of its corporeal owner, past or present; capable of leaving the body far behind, to flash swiftly from place to place; mostly impalpable and invisible, yet also manifesting physical power, and especially appearing to men waking or asleep as a phantasm separate from the body of which it bears the likeness; continuing to exist and appear to men after the death of that body; able to enter into, possess, and act in the bodies of other men, of animals, and even of things. Though this definition is by no means of universal application, it has sufficient generality to be taken as a standard, modified by more or less divergence among any particular people (117, I, pp. 428–429).

The great English scholar expounded his theory across thousands of pages. Well-armed with data, he analyzes the subject of souls that speak, the *sussurrus necromanticus* of witch doctors and mediums, the material description of souls, which are the most subtle or diaphanous part of the body, animals' souls, the souls of inanimate objects, and so on (117, I).

It is worth noting that Herbert Spencer, who exercised so much influence over Tylor, appears inversely to have undergone Tylor's influence shortly after Tylor's animist theories were developed, because in the first part of *Principles of Sociology* (1876), he applies animism to religion. Hankins states that Spencer made fear the primary religious emotion. He derived the idea of the soul from the experiment with shadows, the echo, sleep, and dreams, the idea of ghosts from the soul or alter ego; and he made ancestor worship the universal form of primitive religion. According to Spencer, the mind of primitive man functioned logically at a high level of reasoning, but on false premises because of ignorance of causality in scientific meaning (13, p. 657).

Criticizing animism, Lévy-Bruhl persists in repeating that Tylor's interpretation of data was imposed on him by his position that the mentality of inferior societies obeys the same laws of logic that govern our thought processes. He suggests that this position be abandoned as soon as the mystical and prelogical character of this mentality apepars, and, as a result, the law of participation that governs collective representation. And from that moment, then, the concept of soul would be considered the product of relatively advanced thought processes that are not yet known by inferior societies (72). For that reason, according to Lévy-Bruhl, the mentality of savages is incapable of developing the concept of the soul. As it appears in Tylor, such a concept was the product of his mind, the mind of "an adult, civilized, white man," who is accustomed to formal logic. Arthur Ramos believed that "the animist theory, in spite of its apparent ease in explaining primitive mentality, did nothing but delay achieving a solution to the problem. It would be an explanation of *obscurum per obscurius*, as in the case of opium which makes us sleep because of its sophorific qualities" (101, p. 279). As we stated, on several occasions Ramos found himself obliged to correct the mistakes of his own teacher. We must recognize that even though Nina Rodrigues is considered the precursor of the Afro-Brazilian school of anthropology, he was heavily influenced by animism and evolutionism. This is apparent in *O Animismo Fetichista dos Negros Bahianos* (86).

The Primitive Search for Causality

Although Tylor was surprised by primitive representations, he was even more astonished by the relationship between these representations, that is, the way in which the primitive mentality determines the cause of the phenomena. He finally discovered that whenever there is spatial contiguity and proximity in time, the primitive mentality mistakes coincidences for causes. Seeking a formula to synthesize this discovery, he had recourse to the sophism *juxta hoc, ergo propter hoc; post hoc, ergo propter hoc* ("Next to this, therefore in consequence of this; after this, therefore in consequence of this") (101, p. 278; 104, p. 293; 72).

In his criticism, Lévy-Bruhl roundly denied the causality of primitive causality, that is, the causality of chance. The primitive relation of representations cannot be explained by *juxta hoc, ergo propter hoc*, or coincidence, spatial contiguity, and proximity in time, but by the law of participation, and we will analyze this law later.

Survival

Survival would be a contribution of Tylor to be considered here if, like the others, it were essential for the clarification of the concept of being prelogical. But Lévy-Bruhl does not consider it important. Even though we do so summarily, we do consider it. Through the theory of survivorship, a number of procedures, customs, opinions, etc., which are carried by force of habit to a different social state from their origin, and since then exist as testimonials and examples of an ancient moral and intellectual state from which a new one originated, are explained (117, I). Perhaps it would be worth pointing out that the idea of survivorship in Tylor's deliberations is, in a way, due to the fact that, in spite of being a parallelist, he did not completely deny historical and geographical dispersion. "What today are rules for dispersionists were the exception for the English anthropological school," warns Ramos (98, p. 122).

CONCLUSION

In conclusion, Tylor is a leading voice in the history of social studies because of his impetus in dealing with transcendental problems suggested to him by his understanding of ethnological and folkloric events. His ideas had remarkable acceptance, but they do not resist the criticism of other philosophers of Folklore who dissected them and used them for more congruent results. As Engels has stated so well, "The history of science is the history of the progressive elimination of error, that is to say, of its substitution by a new error, but each one less absurd than the former" (8, p. 117). In fact, it is only now that we can prove easily how forced were Tylor's hypotheses. They permitted "adjustments" each time their main lines encountered obstacles, and they provided deceptive "outs" that gave the appearance of eclecticism. For example, one of these adjustments involved the reason for the quantitative difference of logic. The adjustment was developed as a result of the axiom on the identity of the human spirit, the basis for the theory of convergence. Unable to admit the existence of two logics, Tylor had no other recourse than to broaden his theory by explaining why the primitive finds causes where we only find coincidence, or he speaks of the "duality of the ego" in the primitive. We must, however, not confuse Tylor's discoveries with the explanations that justify them. The adjustments are in the explanations; but the discoveries are still valid. Scholars consider the discoveries of the "duality of the ego" and the "ascientific causality" of the primitive notable. What is criticized are Tylor's explanations of these phenomena; for example, the savage's fear of his shadow, and his recourse to coincidence. Today, modern theories of psychology monopolize this subject, and, for that reason, Tylor must be remembered more than ever. The psychological bases of Folklore are found in his work; indeed, the discovery of the duality of the ego led Freud to an understanding of totemism. And without Tylor, Lévy-Bruhl would have been unable to theorize. In short, Edward B. Tylor was a great pioneer in the study of anthropology.

5

On Being Prelogical—
Théodule A. Ribot

Théodule Armand Ribot (1839–1916) appears to have been the first psychologist who wrote about what he called the "logic of the senses." He did so primarily in his study *Logique des Sentiments* (1905), a complement to *La psychologie des sentiments* (1896). Before him, Comte and Stuart Mill had dealt lightly with this topic, calling attention to the paucity of studies concerning it. Ribot observed that he knew of no person who had even attempted to deal with this intricate question (107) and thereby justified for himself the position of precursor.

We will not analyze all his work. As with Tylor, we will only consider the ideas used later by Lévy-Bruhl in his essays on the logic of the senses applied to savages. These principal ideas are: duality of logic; the independence of affective logic from the principle of contradiction; the synthetic character of affective logic; and the coexistence of two logics. In *How Natives Think*, Lévy-Bruhl never revealed precisely the use he made of Ribot. To indicate this use item by item is our effort. It was sufficient for Lévy-Bruhl to advise at the beginning that he had

> . . . received practical help, too, from the fairly large number of psychologists who, following Ribot, aim at showing the importance of the emotional and the motor elements of mental life in general and extending to the intellectual life, properly so called. To quote but two works, both Ribot's *Logique des Sentiments* and Heinrich Maier's *Psychologie des emotionalen Denkens* show how narrow were the limits within which traditional psychology, under the influence of formal logic, sought to confine the life of thought. Mental processes are infinitely more elastic, complex, and subtle,

and they comprise more elements of the psychic life than a too "simplist" intellectualism would allow. Ribot's observations on psychology, therefore, have been very valuable to me (72, pp. 4–5).

RIBOT'S THEORIES

The Duality of Logic

On explaining the duality of logic, Ribot begins by clarifying what he means by "affective life." He states that by this term he means the instincts, tendencies, desires, aversions; those most complex states that are called emotions, such as fear, anger; the passions, that is, the stable and intense emotions (107). His entire thesis consists in affirming the existence of a certain logic in affective life, in proving that fear, love, anger, etc., "rationate," in other words, in defending the rationalization of the instincts. Ribot indicates that the logic of the senses is an effort to make instincts rational. To illustrate this point, Pascal would note that the heart has reasons which reason itself ignores. For this reason, Ribot concludes that there are two logics: "affective logic" (the logic of the senses, logic of prenotions, logic of belief, logic of error, logic of instincts, logic of the heart) (107, pp. 221–226, 230); and "rational logic" (classical logic, traditional logic, Aristotelian logic, the logic of analogy). Rational logic, governed by the rules of analogy (similarity, contrast, contiguity), was what had been known until that time. No one knew any other. Everything opposed to rational logic was sophistry. What Ribot accomplished, then, was the removal of the logic of the senses from the area of sophistry. He stated that there are sophisms which are anything but affective, and affective rationations which are not sophisms. Only in certain cases can the logic of the senses and sophistry be superimposed (107, p. 41).

It is certain that from the rational point of view, the logic of the senses—which can also be called the logic of prenotions—is perpetual sophistry. Its success, when it does occur, is illegitimate and purely the result of chance. The constant use of concepts and value judgments, subjective creations varying according to the individuals and times used, makes it erroneous. The question is to determine if this logic, which has a use since it exists, is to be judged according to the inflexible rules governing its rival (107, p. 221). . . . In reality, each logic occupies a field of its own. They are developed by differ-

ent processes which are determined by the objectives of each. Each
one has its psychology, its conditions of existence, its reason for
being as an expression of two opposing tendencies of human nature.
Such an impartial position is the one that must be adopted by the
psychologist in order to understand them (107, p. 222).

In justifying the use of the term "logic" with the senses, when
it was formerly restricted to the intellect, Ribot maintains that
both have a common base, reason. Consequently, senses can be
linked with "logic." He defines rational by Boole's formula:
"Reasoning is the elimination of the middle term in a system that
has three terms." Reasoning is a nonimmediate operation which
has a single conclusion as its aim; in other words, a process which
involves finding intermediaries which would lead to its final objective. Affective logic, then, is as unified and strives to attain its goal
as rigorously as rational logic. What seems to be discontinuity
results from the processes it uses. Identifying these processes, Ribot
studies them as mechanism and form of the constituent elements of
logic of the senses.

Disregard of Affective Logic for the Principle of Contradiction

In this section on the component elements of the logic of the
senses, it is important to emphasize that contrary to rational logic,
affective logic is not concerned with the principle of contradiction.
Lévy-Bruhl faced the problem from another angle. He accepted the
indifference mentioned by Ribot, but he stated that it only was
present when it was a question of relationship of ideas, and not, as
Ribot would have wanted it, in cases of affective judgment (107, p.
72). In affective logic, it is the relationship of ideas that does not
agree with the principle of contradiction. In other words, affective
logic unites contradictory actions.

Synthetic Character of Affective Logic

Since affective reasoning does not obey the principle of contradiction, it is more synthetic than analytical. This is another of
Ribot's ideas that is used by Lévy-Bruhl. Ribot wanted to point out
that affective reasoning always presupposes, predetermines; it does
not dissect; neither does it analyze, nor reach conclusions; it merely
aspires to a goal. The third step of emotional reasoning, which,
when joined with the first, eliminates the middle step, is not a con-

clusion but an objective, and, in this, the two logics are vastly different. "Rational reasoning aspires to a conclusion while emotional reasoning aspires to an end; that is, it is not oriented to truth but to practical results, and it is always oriented in this direction" (107, p. 65). Affective logic cannot prove phenomena, only justify them. According to it, reasoning is conditioned by the objective. It would not be incorrect, therefore, to call the logic of the senses, the logic of prenotions. It is above all subjective while "intellectual reasoning has only one goal, that of determining objective truth" (107, p. 68). "Emotional reasoning," emphasized Ribot, "is an adaptation to beliefs, desires, and aversions. It is a subjective position" (107, p. 76).

Coexistence of the Two Logics

The two logics, then, do not function in an isolated manner since they coexist in the same mind. As we shall see, Lévy-Bruhl took advantage of Ribot's idea and developed it into what he called the "prelogical," which is nothing less than the logic of the senses, with certain modifications. In several passages of his study, Ribot deals obliquely with coexistence. He says, for example, that "in the concepts or judgments that we call affective, the idea is a secondary element whose sole role is to serve as a *substratum* to the state of conscience, fix it, give a concrete form to the fluidity of the senses, and to state it this way to make it convenient" (107, p. 44). And that even though the subjective element cannot be eliminated from any argument, in proper cases this is so weak as to not be a matter of concern. Or he states,

> Activities so complex as the making of an instrument or the construction of a shanty require supernatural intervention, prayers, sacrifices, incantations, various rites, and magical formulas for the uncivilized being. According to his process of reasoning, these are essential for him to reach his goal. This is the part that pertains to the logic of sentiments; the rest remains still wrapped up in this mishmash (107, p. 39). . . . There are few people indeed, even the most rational, who do not have some external superstitions even though they consider them absurd. We know calm people who feel that the apparition of ghosts or souls is impossible, and who nevertheless are afraid of them in the dark. The learned person who enters his laboratory and leaves his religion on the threshold is an example of this divided spirit (107, p. 72).

Arthur Ramos, as a reviewer of Ribot and Lévy-Bruhl, writes an entire chapter concerning the "survival of primitive structures in logical minds," in which he emphasizes that "the most civilized man does not free himself entirely from these primitive undifferentiated structures," and that, "this primitivism is not solely the prerogative of the savage-primitive, but of the civilized man as well" (101, pp. 332, 333).

Synthesis of Ribot's Contributions

To synthesize these ideas concerning affective logic, logic independent of the law of contradiction, synthetic logic, a priori, subjective and coexistent with formal logic, let us consult Ribot's summation:

> The logic of reason in its correct form is decided by nature and by the subjective order of phenomena, whether these be conjectural or observed, as in a discovery. It is made up of intellectual states (perception, images, and concepts above all) freed as much as possible from emotional biases.
>
> Logic of the senses is governed by the subjective nature of the reasoner who hopes to postulate an opinion, a belief for himself and others. Its origin stems from a positive or negative desire which seeks an appearance of proof. It is primarily made up of "values," that is, variable concepts or judgments in accordance with the inclinations of the will and the senses. Among these "values," the predetermined objectives determine the acceptance of some and the rejection of others.
>
> As a conjectural conclusion, like the end of an illness, a business deal . . . rational reasoning breaks the problem down into its components—the constitution of the sick, the seriousness of the symptoms, the skill of the doctor, the possibility of painstaking care, etc.—and the final result is the totality of partial conclusions. In business, an impartial examination of the facts is conducted, exact, complete with data. Calculations are accomplished on the pro and con over a period of time, according to Franklin's method. These are later compared, counterbalanced, and balanced, in order to reach a conclusion. In the same way, in conclusions concerning actions—for example determining the character of a person—the intellectual study analyzes, breaks the problem down into its component parts, deduces, induces, and from the sum of the partial judgments, reaches a final judgment.
>
> In logic of the senses, on the other hand, the conclusion is virtually determined ahead of time. If reasoning is conjectural, it depends on the optimistic or pessimistic, daring or timid, hopeful

or doubtful character of the one who is reasoning. If it is a case of valuation as in the preceding case, it depends on a stable or flighty, sympathetic or averse, confident or distrustful nature that determines the value judgment. The synthesis of these values by accumulation or by rank has the appearance, and produces the illusion, of a *demonstration*. Rational logic, in fact, many times proceeds in the same way, the conclusion being determined ahead of time. A theorem, a mathematical problem considered solved, a principle of physics—and the reason is dedicated to his proof. But the fundamental difference between both cases does not need to be demonstrated (107, pp. 78–80).

CONCLUSION

In conclusion, we can state that Ribot's proof of the existence of two logics was a fundamental point of departure for Lévy-Bruhl. He applied Ribot's ideas to ethnography and folklore and discovered that most of them fell into the framework of the logic of the senses. On the other hand, Ribot's affective reasoning is nothing more than the ascientific causality of Tylor. In comparing them, it will be apparent that Ribot was so radical that he did not even permit those "adjustments" of Tylor to which we have already referred. He did not admit the matter of two quantitatively different logics, and Lévy-Bruhl almost agreed with him about this. Ribot's ideas were later to become almost indispensable to Freud. The psychoanalyst's framework is erected, to a considerable degree, on the theory of affective logic.

In our Folklore, especially, Ribot's theories are basic for conceptualization of the "prelogical" or "plebeian" characteristics of the folkloric act.* Using already known elements, this conceptualization can be structured in the following manner: (1) The plebeian act results from the logic of the senses or the logic of prenotions, the logic of belief, the logic of error, the logic of the instincts, or the logic of the heart. (2) The plebeian does not obey the logical rational principle of contradiction because, in his causal relationships, he explains results by causes that are specifically contradictory. In other words, he explains the results without making use of rules of analogy of rational logic: similarity, contrast, and con-

*Translator's Note: Plebeian. In the Spanish Edition: Vulgo, Vulgar.

tiguity. (3) The plebeian presupposes and predetermines. He does not discompose and analyze, nor does he reach conclusions. His reasoning leads to an end instead of a conclusion. Because of this, he does not verify phenomena, he only justifies them. His logic is subjective and is not dedicated to the discovery of objective truth. In summary, his logic is synthetic. (4) The plebeian individual (folk individual, *vulgo*) is and is not folk at the same time. This is because the logic of feelings coexists with the logic of reason in the same mentality, even though the individual may be closer at times to prelogical thinking than not. As Lévy-Bruhl points out, prelogical thinking is especially evident when the individual acts collectively.

6

On Being Prelogical—
Lucien Lévy-Bruhl

And so we come to Lucien Lévy-Bruhl (1857–1939). He has made
many theoretical contributions to the social sciences. We will, however, only consider here those concerning the primitive mind.
These are: collective representations, an idea that owes much to
Ribot; mysticism, which is a criticism of Tylor's animism; the law
of participation, which discusses Tylor's explanation of primitive
causality; and, finally, the prelogical mentality, an idea that criticizes Tylor's theory of convergence. Bear in mind at the outset that
the French scholar's classical work on these matters is called *Les
fonctions mentales dans les sociétés inferieures (How Natives
Think)* (72), and that the methodology that guides him is Durkheim's comparative method, which, as we saw, was also used by
Tylor. Contrary to Tylor, Lévy-Bruhl developed his thesis with the
knowledge of the psychological discoveries that came after Ribot
and Henrich Maier.

LÉVY-BRUHL'S THEORIES

Collective Representations

According to Lévy-Bruhl, the primitive individual develops
"collective representations." He states that he uses the term "representation" in its present psychological meaning: pure or almost
pure perception. In other words, representation is an intellectual
or cognitive phenomenon, par excellence. According to psychological rules, other perceptions are emotional or affective and
motor; and they are not representations. Lévy-Bruhl states that

only the civilized individual develops true representations, because he perceives the image or idea of an object with little influence from affective or motor elements. Representations of primitive man are not the same as for civilized man, because these are saturated with affective elements. And since primitive man develops these affective elements when he forms groups, his representations should be labeled "collective." With the exception of strictly personal emotions resulting from the immediate reaction of the being, nothing is more socialized among primitive men than emotions (72).

Mysticism

If representations of primitive men are not pure, within the specific meaning of the term, they

> express, or rather imply, not only that the primitive actually has an image of the object in his mind, and thinks its real, but also that he has some hope or fear connected with it, that some definite influence emanates from it, or is exercised upon it. This influence is a virtue, an occult power which varies with objects and circumstances, but is always real to the primitive and forms an integral part of his representation. If I were to express in one word the general peculiarity of the collective representations which play so important a part in the mental activity of undeveloped peoples, I should say that this mental activity was a *mystic* one. In default of a better, I shall make use of this term—not referring thereby to the religious mysticism of our communities, which is something entirely different, but employing the word in the strictly defined sense in which "mystic" implies belief in forces and influences and actions which, though imperceptible to sense, are nevertheless real (72, pp. 24–25).
>
> . . . It is not correct to maintain, as is frequently done, that primitives associate occult powers, magic properties, a kind of soul or vital principle with all the objects which affect their senses or strike their imagination, and that their perceptions are surcharged with animistic beliefs. It is not a question of *association*. The mystic properties with which things and beings are imbued form an integral part of the idea to the primitive, who views it as a synthetic whole (72, p. 31).

Only mysticism, says Lévy-Bruhl, has the power to lead us to an understanding of the dichotomy of "ego" and "nonego," the preliminary dichotomy used by Tylor to explain animism; a phenomenon in which "ego" of primitive men is confused with objects of the external world, plants, animals, and things. Therefore, in the collective representations of primitive mentalities, the objects, beings, phenomena, in a manner incomprehensible to us, while being themselves, can at the same time be something different from themselves. In an even less understandable way, they emit and receive power, virtues, qualities, and mystical actions that are felt by others without their changing their own nature. He goes on to say that this is how the Trumaí of Brazil claim they are aquatic animals and the Bororó boast about being red parrots. He summarizes that all totemically organized societies have collective representations of the same type, presupposing a similarity of identity between the individuals of a totemic group and their totem (72).

For greater clarity let us read Arthur Ramos, who also reaches the same conclusion.

> Inanimate objects in nature are considered "alive" and "animate" by primitive man, not because they possess a "soul,"—a "spirit," or something that makes them animate, but because savage man's perception is *mystical*, that is, it is directly tied to those emotional and motor elements which orient and direct primitive man's attitudes toward them. Primitive man can animate things with "spirits," not by a philosophy developed especially for this purpose, but because his mentality is *mystical*. . . . Finally, for primitive man, all things in nature appear cloaked with a mystical character, not because they shelter hidden spirits, invisible beings who manipulate everything skillfully and intelligently, as is postulated by the animist hypothesis. The explanation rests in that the outside world is perceived by primitive man through a distinct mentality. It is not that inanimate objects are alive and endowed with all these characteristics, but the psyche of the savage, filled with emotional and motor elements, transforms objective reality (101, pp. 184–285).

Law of Participation

Collective representations and mysticism help us to understand the law of participation since these ideas are incorporated in their development. Briefly, the law of participation, as understood by Lévy-Bruhl, establishes the existence of a relation of collective representations developed under the influence of mysticism, and independent from a contiguous sequence, that is, from physical proximity.

The law of participation, therefore, criticized Tylor's explanation of primitive causality, as the concepts of collective representation and mysticism were critical of animism. From our vantage point, we may have the impression that Lévy-Bruhl's work was developed to contradict Tylor's. The truth is that the French school of anthropology builds on the English school and succeeds in examining the topic of primitive mentalities more deeply.

Examining the concepts of the law of participation in detail, we will recall that Tylor explained the rules of causality among primitive men by means of coincidences, that is, by events that were merely spatially contiguous or temporally near each other. These events were the causes of the consequences observed. An antecedent was sought in space or in time that justified the consequences. *(Post hoc, ergo propter hoc; juxta hoc, ergo propter hoc.)* Reiterating his ideas, phenomena were only joined by their physical proximity and their location in time. For Lévy-Bruhl, this was explaining causality by chance. He emphatically denied that chance existed in primitive causality. He believed that the relationship of cause and effect among savages develops as a result of the action of mystical powers, thus voiding the hypothesis of physical proximity and location in time. He labeled "law of participation" the relationship he conceived. He indicated that for this reason, and for want of a better term, he would call *law of participation* the very principle of primitive mentality governing the relations and prerelations of these representations (72).

Examples are numerous in Lévy-Bruhl's works. He writes of the accounts of early voyagers concerning the relation of representations that appeared strange and inexplicable to them. From a traveler among the indigenous of North America:

> One evening, when talking about the animals of the country, I wanted to let them know that we had rabbits and leverets in France, and I showed them to them by making the shadow on the wall in the firelight. It happened quite by chance that they caught more fish than usual the next morning; they believed that the shadow pictures I had made for them were the cause of this, and they begged me to do this every evening and to teach them how, a thing which I refused to do, as I would not minister to this foolish superstition of theirs (72, p. 58).

From Doctor Eduard Pechuël-Loesche, a traveler in Africa:

After the Catholic missionaries had landed, there was a scarcity of rain, and the plantations were suffering from drought. The people at once took it into their heads that this was the fault of these clerics, and especially due to the long robes they wore, for such had never been seen before. There was besides a white horse which had recently been landed, and it had prevented trading, and occasioned many troublesome discussions. A contractor had a great deal of trouble because he had replaced the pole of native wood which was badly warped, upon which his flag was erected, by an upright mast which had just been imported. A shiny mackintosh coat, an unusual hat, a rocking-chair, any instrument whatever, can give rise to disquieting suspicions. The entire coast population may be disturbed at the sight of a sailingship with unfamiliar rigging, or a steamer which has one more funnel than the others. If anything vexatious should occur, it is at once attributed to something unusual that has taken place (72, pp. 56–57).

When considering such actions, Lévy-Bruhl insists that it would be a mistake to explain them by saying that primitive men apply the principle of causality without judgment and confuse the antecedent with the cause. Mysticism fundamentally controls the relationship of collective representations. There is a "law of participation" which causes primitive man to ascribe causative powers for favorable or unfavorable events as in the cited example of the shadow of fingers and the priest's cassock. Casuality of causality does not exist then. Attributing the responsibility for any action at all to the origin of another action is a process governed by the "law of participation." It is not an arbitrary process subject purely to chance. Lévy-Bruhl writes that he does not try to explain these relationships by the weakness of primitive man's intellectual powers, by the association of ideas, by an ingenious application of the principle of causality or by the sophism *post hoc, ergo propter hoc*. In other words, his mental activities are not relegated to a form inferior to ours (72).

Lévy-Bruhl also cites examples against the condition of "immediate precedence," so beloved by Tylor. He believes that it exists, but that it is not always necessary. He describes how primitive men are at times incapable of conceiving the sequential relationships that are immediately apparent, and cites Martin Dobritzhofer on the Abipones:

A wound inflicted with a spear often gapes so wide that it affords
ample room for life to go out and death to come in; yet if the man
dies of the wound, they really believe him killed, not by a weapon,
but by the deadly arts of the jugglers. . . . They are persuaded that
the juggler will be banished from amongst the living, and made to
atone for their relation's death, if the heart and tongue be pulled
out of the dead man's body immediately after his decease, roasted
at the fire, and given to dogs to devour. Though so many hearts
and tongues are devoured, and they never observe any of the
jugglers die, yet they religiously adhere to the custom of their
ancestors by cutting out the hearts and tongues of infants and adults
of both sexes, as soon as they have expired (72, p. 60).

The law of participation is, then, the relationship of collective
representations functioning not by chance (mystical participation)
and independent from an immediate temporal sequence. Lévy-
Bruhl then enumerates the categories or diverse forms where this
rule or law appears: contact, transfer, sympathy, action at a distance, et cetera. As an illustration,

In many aggregates of an undeveloped type the abundance of game,
fish, or fruit, the regularity of the seasons, and the rainfall are
connected with the performance of certain ceremonies by individuals destined thereto; or to the presence or to the well-being
of a sacred personality who possesses a special mystic power. Or yet
again, the newborn child feels the effects of everything its father
does, what he eats, etc. The Indian, out hunting or engaged in
warfare, is fortunate or unfortunate according to whether his wife,
left behind in the camp, eats, or abstains from eating, certain
foods, or is doing or not doing certain things (72, pp. 62–63).

The Prelogical Mentality

His observations and Ribot's observations before him lead Lévy-
Bruhl to a fourth theory, that of the prelogical mentality, and in
so doing to a criticism of Tylor's theory of convergence, a denial
that a common mental state exists for primitive and civilized man
(quod semper, quod ubique, quod ab omnibus). What separates
the "white, adult, civilized" man from primitive man, says Lévy-
Bruhl, is not the quantitative difference of thought, but, more
properly, differences of a qualitative order. Aristotle's rules of traditional, classical, analogic logic are not always valid for the savage.
Lévy-Bruhl observes that the mental processes of savage man al-

ways have their own rules whenever they are collective, and the first and most common is the law of participation (72). According to this rule, savage man does not reason by Aristotelian logic, that is, the rules of analogy: similarity, contrast, contiguity—like recalls like, largeness calls to mind smallness, the professor of Folklore calls to mind the student of Folklore (75, p. V). As a consequence, therefore, of the laws of participation, savage man does not develop analogies in an Aristotelian manner. He is only capable of developing inconsistent analogies: shadows to fishes, missionaries to rain, wounds causing death to witch doctors, and so on. Rules of inconsistency and the rules of participation coexist in his mentality. Because of this, Lévy-Bruhl concludes that there is a basis for primitive man's mind to be characterized as mystical (72). It is prelogical since it develops relationships of collective representations that are contradictory, but to the savage's logic are analogical.

Prelogicalness does not exclude "Aristotelian logic" and, therefore, must not be considered "antilogical" nor "alogical" nor does it indicate chronological preference. Prelogic and traditional logic coexist in the same savage mentality.

> In the mentality of primitive peoples, the logical and prelogical are not arranged in layers and separated from each other like oil and water in a glass. They permeate each other, and the result is a mixture which is a very difficult matter to differentiate. Since the laws of logic absolutely exclude, in our own thought, everything that is directly contrary to itself, we find it hard to get accustomed to a mentality in which the logical and prelogical can be co-existent and make themselves equally perceptible in mental processes (72, p. 89).

G. Van der Leew, a successor to Lévy-Bruhl, faithful to the scholar's wishes to prevent terciary meanings for the term "prelogical," proposed substituting "heterological" for it (in 101, p. 289).

Going deeper into the subject of the differences between logical and prelogical mentalities, Lévy-Bruhl points out that prelogical mentalities are essentially synthetic and as such do not place a value on experience. They do not conduct prior analysis. They do not obey the rules of contradiction; nor do they develop, separate, compare, classify, or in other ways perform the mental processes appropriate to traditional logic. He states,

What strikes us first of all is that prelogical mentality is little given to analysis. Undoubtedly in a certain sense every act of thought is synthetic, but when it is a question of logical thought this synthesis implies, in nearly every case, a previous analysis. Relations are expressed by judgments only after the food for thought has first been well digested, and subjected to elaboration, differentiation, and classification. Judgment deals with ideas which have been rigidly defined, and these are themselves the proof and product of previous logical processes. Prelogical mentality is essentially synthetic. By this I mean that the syntheses which compose it do not imply previous analyses of which the result has been registered in definite concepts [. . .] (72, p. 90).

Let us also read the following rather lucid paragraph of Arthur Ramos concerning this matter:

There is a fundamental difference in the intrinsic mechanism of logical and prelogical mentalities. While rational logic operates by means of analysis and consecutive synthesis and deals with abstract or concrete concepts developed by prior experiences by means of analysis, separation, classification . . . prelogical reasoning functions in a different way. It does not separate, nor compare; nor does it conduct prior analysis, nor follow the rules of contradiction (101, p. 287).

We have stated that as a result of being prelogical as contrasted with being logical, primitive mentalities have proved impervious to experience, are insensible to contradiction, and are a priori; that is, they allow for preconceptions and prerelations. In the case of the Abipones, experience should teach them that tearing out the hearts and tongues of the dead, roasting them over the fire, and then throwing them to the dogs to cause the witch doctor's death is nothing more than an innocuous practice since the Abipones never saw a witch doctor's death result from this ritual. Indifferent to experience, however, they continue to tear out the hearts and tongues, roast them over the fire, throw them to the dogs to cause the death of the witch doctor. Experience, then, has insufficient power to redirect them from their error and to teach them (72).

Synonyms were also developed for the term "synthetic" in the meaning of the word used here. One proposed by Lévy-Bruhl's successors was the term "asyntactic" (101, p. 289). By "asyntactic," they hoped to develop the idea of a synthesis developed by processes different from the dialectic synthesis of civilized mentalities. The thesis opposes the antithesis in cognitive representations, and synthesis arises from this opposition, which in its turn develops a new thesis. And the process does not stop. The synthesis of prelogical representations being different should more properly be called "asyntactical."

The topic of prelogical mentalities is extensive, and Lévy-Bruhl explains it in beautiful, clear, objective, and scientific prose. We have here attempted to summarize, didactically, the basic ideas of the great French scholar. Possibly this is the first time in the Americas that they have been applied to folklore. In any case, we do hope the reader will consult the entire work.

SYNTHESIS OF LÉVY-BRUHL'S THEORIES

The theory of Tylor's English school of anthropology dealing with primitive mentalities upholds the validity of traditional logic in life experiences of primitive man. It specifies the separation of the ego and nonego by developing the theory of animism, and establishes the fact that primitive causality is controlled by proximity in space and time. The French school of anthropology, directed by Lévy-Bruhl, analyzes and criticizes Tylor's theory, postulate by postulate, applying the results of this analysis and criticism to the phenomena of perception and representation, as well as to other psychic faculties such as memory, attention, abstraction, and generalization.

The results of Lévy-Bruhl's close study of Tylorian theory are his development of the fundamental concepts of collective representation, mysticism, the law of participation, and the prelogical state of the primitive mind. In the course of arriving at the concepts of collective representation and mysticism, Lévy-Bruhl dismisses Tylor's idea of animism, and he further conceives the "law of participation" as a contradiction of Tylor's explanation of the primitive causal relationship. But Lévy-Bruhl is very much indebted to Tylor for his idea of the prelogical mentality, which developed essentially out of opposition to Tylor's axiom affirming the identity of a human intellect completely similar to itself from the logical point of view and at all times and places (72).

Because Tylor was directly influenced by Spencer and, according to Lévy-Bruhl, accepted his views on evolutionism, Tylor attempted to study primitive man with the logic of "white, adult, civilized man," and this might have been the reason for the many theoretical errors of the English school of anthropology. It did not take into account the existence of two logics, and so erected its monumental structure on an unsupportable foundation. Lévy-Bruhl, therefore, concluded that Spencerian evolutionism was at the root of Tylor's misjudgments.

CRITICISM OF LÉVY-BRUHL

Tylor, obviously, is not the only scholar susceptible to criticism. Lévy-Bruhl's turn soon came. Among his critics are such scholars as Mauss, Weber, Boas, Paul Rivet, Aupiais, Raymond Lenoir, Léon Brunschvigg, Charles Blondel, Émile Meyerson, Durkheim, Bergson, Kroeber, Schmidt, Lowie, Pinar de la Boullaye, A. A. Goldenweiser, and Richard Thurnwald (11, p. 39; 101, pp. 282, 283; 104, p. 415; 76). We are also familiar with his own self-criticism published posthumously by Maurice Leenhardt under the title *Les Carnets* (73). Concerning these, consult the excellent reviews of Imbelloni (63) and Florestán Fernandes (47). Why then did we devote so much space to the great French scholar? The answer is obvious, for the same reason that we did so for Tylor. We find that some of his theories and the ideas they control are still in order today.

Other Works by Lévy-Bruhl

Once the fundamental structure of his theory was developed in *Les fonctions mentales dans les sociétés inférieurs* (1910) (*How Natives Think*) Lévy-Bruhl continued its development and growth in other works: *La Mentalité Primitive* (1922), *L'ame primitive* (1927), *Le surnaturel et la nature dans la pensée primitive* (1931), and *L'experience mystique et les symbols chez les primitifs* (1938). Using the comparative method, he dedicated thirty years to this task.

Development of Prelogical Mentality and Educational Folklore

Through education, the mystical and prelogical mentality can evolve, and, in developing, can become consistently more logical. As we see it, this is a topic that belongs to educational folklore, or as Hegel would say, "intellectual freedom." Lévy-Bruhl, in his explanation, however, merely considers it a problem in taking advantage of experience. He sees the prelogical mentality evolving only when primitive synthesis, the prerelations of collective representations, dissolves, bit by bit, and disappears; in other words, if experience and logical needs overcome the rule of participation. Submitting to these needs, then, thought will begin to change, to free itself, and to become relevant. Rather complex intellectual processes will become possible. The logical mechanism which will join, step by step, with thinking, is at once as much a necessary condition of its freedom as the indispensable element of its progress (72).

Among those who have written on this topic, Afrânio Peixoto, a colleague of Ramos, called to his generation in Brazil as loudly as Nina Rodrigues' disciple, that *he did not want to believe but to know.* (Peixoto, in 99, p. VIII.) And Roger Garaudy wrote, "Truly man is ruled by laws of reality while he does not know about them. He is controlled by nature and a society already created without knowing the laws of his own evolution. But as soon as he begins to understand the nature of these phenomena, he is capable of foreseeing them and modifying them according to his rules" (8, p. 127). And Paul Saintyves in France states: "Folklore would not have a place among the people if every individual had a higher education which freed him from all prejudice and superstition" (25, p. 14). Ramos even contended that Brazil's *curandeirismo* problem would not be solved by jails, but by means of the "slow education of the circles where the urban folk medicine men operate and the development of correct norms of thinking and rational logic in opposition to these mystical and prelogical and undisciplined practices" (102, p. 77).

We have returned to this topic in *Folklore y Educación.** European clergymen thought that they had freed Brazilian Negroes and Indians from their fetishism, not suspecting the possibility of its prelogical survival in a disguised form. They were victims of the celebrated catechetical illusion mentioned by Nina Rodrigues.

*Translator's Note: See *Folklore y Educación,* 1st edition. Quito: Casa de la Cultura Ecuatoriana, 1961, p. 315. 2nd Spanish edition, Buenos Aires: Editorial Omeba, 1969.

Fundamentally, the Afro-Brazilians revered their old African *orixás* even though they were apparently ready to simulate Catholic rituals.

Validity of Lévy-Bruhl's Theory for Other Psychic Phenomena

Up to this point, we have dealt with Lévy-Bruhl's theory only as it applied to the phenomena of perception and representation. It is worth noting, nevertheless, that it is valid for other psychic phenomena, such as memory, attention, abstraction, and generalization. Dealing with such topics, however, would require extensive discussions that are not really germane to our objectives.

CONCLUSIONS APPLICABLE TO FOLKLORE

At this point, the reader will have, on his own, developed several conclusions concerning folklore. Let us, however, synthesize ours in our own way. The prelogical or plebeian act and prelogical, plebeian, or folk individual have the following characteristics: (1) The prelogical individual develops "collective representations," that is, representations that are not purely cognitive or rational but are heavily loaded with emotional and motivating traits. We could say, as did Ribot, that the prelogical individual, while in the prelogical state, is governed by logic of the emotions, which is a logic containing rational traits, but, above all, affective ones. (2) The primitive or plebeian dualism of the ego or alter ego (the latter represented by shadows, animals, plants, and so on) must not be explained by simple association as does Tylor's animistic theory, but by Lévy-Bruhl's mystical theory. According to it, the alter ego is not a disconnected association of the individual. It is not chosen at random. On the contrary, it is a result of the same collective representation and is closely bound to it. In other words, it is a projection of the individual; it emanates from the individual and is always bound to him and changes only when his emotions change. (3) Primitive or plebeian causality must not be explained by Tylor's principle of spatial contiguity and proximity of time, but rather by Lévy-Bruhl's law of participation. This law states that primitive causality is achieved by relations of collective representations among themselves, and that these relations only function under mysticism, without the need of an immediate sequence or proximity of time. (4) Differences in reasoning between the primitive or plebeian individual and the civilized individual must not be explained by having recourse to Tylor's ideas of minds that are only quantitatively identifiable. Rather, says Lévy-Bruhl, they should be considered as minds that are qualitatively different. By primitive mentalities, we then mean those that do not comply with the Aristotelian principle of contradiction, because they are controlled by the prelogical law of participation. As Ribot had observed, the prelogical mind is synthetic because it does not obey the rules of contradiction of classical logic. In other words, it does not know how to break down, to analyze, to reach conclusions, but prefers presupposing, predetermining, and justifying. Finally, it places no value on experience. (5) These two logics, rational and affective, coexist in the individual. That is, the individual simultaneously thinks like the folk and does not think like the folk. There are special occasions when he is, above all, prelogical. These are collective activities, when many plebeians are gathered together for a social activity appropriate to the culture, such as a funeral or a feast. (6) There exists an effective way of helping the plebeian free his mind from his prelogical thinking, but this method is not a part of Folklore; it belongs to the field of education.

7

On Being Prelogical—
Sigmund Freud

In Freud, we find yet another substantial contribution on the subject of primitive mentalities. At the present time, he is even more essential to Folklore's development than the other scholars we have mentioned.

Because Freud was a neurologist, we must be prepared for a complete change of nomenclature when dealing with the characteristics of the primitive act or with its causes and processes. But different labels must not becloud the strong ties Freud had to his predecessors.

Freud recognized that the primitive act is, in fact, characterized by its failure to comply with logic's rule of contradiction, the predominance of emotional content and motives over cognitive content, for causal ends and not conclusions, for its presuppositions, and its experimental invalidity. Instead of a prelogical or primitive act, he called it narcissistic or magical, and he did not delay in collecting these characteristics under key terms just as Ribot and Lévy-Bruhl did with "collective representations" and "synthetic character."

On investigating the causes of the plebeian act and the psychic bases leading to the performance of these acts, Freud handles the same kind of ideas that were the *leitmotiv* of concepts such as "mysticism," "law of participation," and "prelogical mentality." His explanations, however, are quite different. In general, they originate in what he called the "libido"; and it is in this concept that his great originality lies.

Psychoanalysis, then, explains not only the origin of ordinary acts, that is, acts that are erroneously logical in folklore, but it contains elements that also explain the origin of nonprelogical folkloric acts. Certain songs, tales, and popular art, for example, can be clearly placed within the bounds of cognition or rationality. While Tylor and Lévy-Bruhl do not use them at all, Freud's wonderful theory of psychoanalysis discovers why they exist. Through it, then, the folkloric act may or may not be a product of prelogical mentality, but it always is the product of certain psychic states predisposed to its development. Freud's contribution, then, is in many ways important for Folklore: (1) It explains the origin of magic acts; (2) it describes the qualities of the plebeian man; (3) it explains the origin of folkloric acts that are not produced by the common people; (4) it describes the qualities of the individual who is not from the populace but may still be the bearer of folkloric acts.

These considerations lead us to place restrictions on the preciseness of the very term "folklore" itself, since folkloric science is not only the study of knowledge of the folk (or plebeian mind, or prelogical, or primitive individual) but also of the knowledge of those minds that are generally not plebeian. If this was not so, the field of education would not have anything to gain from folklore and would denounce it in its entirety.

INTRODUCTION TO THE PSYCHOANALYSIS OF FOLKLORE

There are many psychoanalytical ideas that are of particular interest to folklore; but since the subject of the psychoanalysis of folklore is a chapter so vast that it can only be dealt with comprehensively in a special study,* here our objective is only to show Freud's contribution to the conceptualization of the prelogical condition of the folkloric act.

Freud's studies cover considerable ground, beginning with his consideration of the mental structure, including the topic of energy that makes this structure operate, and concluding with the mechanisms that are observable in it for the regulation of this energy (55). To explain the concept of mental energy, Freud had recourse to the concept of the libido, developed in part by Albert

*Translator's Note: See the author's *Folklore and Psychoanalysis.*

Moll in 1898. This term equates with the idea of hunger but as it applies to sex; it is a type of sexual hunger (53). Since biology uses the term "sexual instinct" in this case, it can then be said that libido is a term for the theory of instincts appropriate for the designation of the dynamic expression of sexuality (48). This dynamic expression is characterized by three well-defined phases: the oral, the anal, and the genital. Only the last one, which comes with the advent of puberty and corresponds to the adult years, was known. The majority of scientists during the past century had not conceived of the existence of infant sexuality. They only accepted as sexual acts those that were appropriate for reproduction. Freud's recognition of infant sexuality was one of his great contributions.

The libido is oral in its first stage, because the body's maximum erogeneity is in the mouth. Freud believed that erogeneity is the power of a part of the body to dispatch to the psychic state stimuli that are sexually exciting (49). This maximum erogeneity develops in the mouth through continual oral excitation. Sucking a pacifier is the highest free expression of the primitive libido's desires. He sucks the pacifier, the thumb, and even the big toe. Freud classifies this activity as frankly autoerotic because the child does not suck the thumb or any other part of someone's else's body, but only his own. The object of his libido is found in himself. Oral libido is, therefore, an autoerotic libido. With the growth of teeth, sucking is replaced by chewing and, consequently, the mother snatches her breast away from the child. With weaning, the child finds himself deprived of his erogenous pleasures, and for ethical and social reasons, he is deprived of his pacifier. In some respects, the man/woman and infant/pacifier relationships have much in common.

Hindered in this way, sexual energy desperately seeks other outlets. The child does not know how to control his drives because his representations are not fully cognitive but rather predominantly motor. He is then led blindly by sexual energy, and where new erogenic zones develop, the experiences of the first stage will be repeated. In this interval of anxiety and doubt, attention is directed to the anal stimulation produced by the passage of excrement. And a day arrives when the anus becomes an authentic erogenic region. Pleasure comes from holding in the feces, which are equal to the pacifier. The child cherishes them because they produce the desired sensation. He loves them; he touches them and covers himself with them. The enemas that are used to overcome constipation in turn become pleasures, that is, new stimulation, even though they are painful. But as is logical, for ethical and social reasons, parents and other adults again prevent these heavenly dreams. And the drama of deprivation begins again.

This continues until one day the boy and the girl discover at the same time that one is different from the other; that he has "something" that she doesn't have. Enormous doubts develop in both of them; they want to know if these differences are common, and it is difficult for them to imagine how adults appear. They exhaust the patience of their parents with persistent and endless questions. This is a typical phase of children's curiosity. The fact is that sexual organs occupy the center of their attention. They hold back their urine for pure pleasure, and they excite themselves in other ways, giving way to masturbation's reign. But still this is autoerotic, the successor to the first stage of libido. The last step remains to be taken, and it is perhaps the most difficult of all: the discovery that there is something better than autoeroticism, and it is outside of the individual, that is, in another individual. The memory of the mother leads the adolescent, little by little, to the arms of a woman, a woman who resembles his mother. Thus the libido becomes genital, or, in other words, an objective libido.

Based on this structure of the libido, Freud then proceeds to explain various kinds of questions that were the most pressing of his period. He attributes the phenomenon of "collective representations" in folklore to "narcissism." These Lévy-Bruhl explained by "mysticism," and Tylor by "animism." Narcissism is nothing more than an autoerotic exaggeration. Autoeroticism creates situations making it possible to overvalue the ego (49). This egocentric "hyperesteem" develops in such a way that the individual even comes to believe that the ego can overcome the universe, can dominate everything, and that it is sufficient to think of an action for it to be effective. In Freud's words, the individual believes in the "omnipotence of his ideas." Because he loves himself so much, he cannot admit that death is final. His ego will survive and, in addition, if he so desires, he can order his ego to pass into another body, even into another species, and so produce from a single ego, two egos. Because this Freudian explanation is biological (since it deals with the instincts) as well as philosophical, it seems more convincing than the other theories we have discussed. In "collective representations," the individual is narcissistic. Magic, as a typical expression of collective representations, is, consequently, a narcissistic product. By the same token, in psychoanalytical folklore, magic is explained by narcissism (52). It is the same prelogical magic that so concerned Tylor and Lévy-Bruhl.

In larger terms, magic can be considered as a sexual phenomenon. The "omnipotence of ideas" also acquires the status of being one characteristic among others, of the prelogical condition of the folklore act and the folk individual. Freud establishes within this criterion categories of magic: magic as such, animism, religion, fetishism, totemism, and tabooism. It is well to point out that his concept of animism is different from Tylor's old concept.

Besides narcissism, there are certain phenomena tied in with the libido that Freud uses to complement the explanation of magic folkloric acts such as the Oedipus complex. The Oedipus complex is the psychic conflict that takes place in the individual when he progresses from autoeroticism to projected eroticism. We already noted that the male's first tendency was toward his own mother. To transfer this tendency to another woman and to yield the mother to the father is what constitutes the so-called Oedipus conflict. While the Oedipus complex survives, the individual is autoerotic and frequently strongly narcissistic. In the Oedipus conflict, he has hostile feelings toward his father and respectfully loving but censured feelings for his mother. The mother is a beloved but taboo object. Until the individual successfully conquers the Oedipus complex, the familiar conflict continues. To satisfy himself with his mother is impossible and to kill his father, his worst enemy, is difficult (53, 48, 50). Using the Oedipus complex, Freud completes the explanation of certain "collective representations." The phenomena of relations of collective representations Lévy-Bruhl explains by means of the "law of participation," Freud explains by his theory of the Oedipus complex. Let us take as examples, an unforeseen event and the death of a wounded person. Primitively, an unforeseen event is attributed to the totem who was offended. The death of the wounded person is the totem's punishment. These are but two examples of relations of perfectly contradictory representations, not associative, and, furthermore, impervious to the lessons of experience. How does the social psychoanalyst explain them? Freud believes that the relations of representations occur because the totem is the father figure, that is the father according to the configuration given him by the son under the Oedipus complex. When the participants in totemic ceremonies destroy the totem, they are unconsciously causing the symbolic death of the father because of his privileges in the family.

The Oedipus complex also explains folkloric taboo. In the situation of attraction and rejection toward the mother, the child arrives at a real understanding of his feelings of dilemma: to love and to flee, to be or not to be. He finally denies himself everything he wants passionately. Freud says that in effect we do not see the need of prohibiting what no one wishes to accomplish. The object of desire is what must be strictly prohibited (52).

8

Conclusions on the Folkloric Act

ON BEING PRELOGICAL—SUMMATION OF PRELOGICAL CONDITION

We have finally conceptualized the prelogical act, but there are yet other areas to explore to achieve the general conceptualization of folklore. Before going any further, let us look back, get a general view, and make one final summation of the prelogical condition.

The Prelogical Act and the Folk Individual

The four theories we have discussed follow a chronologically ascending trajectory. At the present, they still contribute to the discovery of fundamental data. It is not possible then to refute them fully. Each one of them possesses some assets. The portion of these assets relative to the prelogical act, which is the portion of most concern to folklore, clearly confirms that it is an act containing more affective and motor elements than cognitive elements, and that it always takes place when there are gatherings of people. As representations, however, these acts are not manifested *ex nihilo*. There are psychic links that cause their occurrence and intimately tie them to the thinking person, whether or not the phenomena is thought of as mystical or as a consequence of the libido. These acts are not manifested *ex nihilo* either as relations of representations. There are psychological factors that are the origin and control of prelogical causality whether or not the phenomenon is called "law of participation," or an effect of the libido. In summary, such an act is a subjective act; that is, it is not dissected by the individual who performs it. It is not analyzed nor are inferences reached from it, because synthetic (asyntactic) or not, it is not the result of experience. If we subject the prelogical act to the screen of cognitive reasoning, we immediately discover its inconsistency, its inconclusiveness, its characteristics leading to error, its vulgarity. The one who performs the act, however, does not see it the way we do. And because of this, he continues to preserve it. He accepts it not because he understands it, but rather because he believes in it, has faith in it. When this faith begins to disintegrate under the stimulation of education, the performer of prelogical acts enters into a period of conflict that eventually leads him to freedom. The path of knowledge is the path of freedom. No one, then, is permanently prelogical or primitive. There are no plebeian people, no folk people, but rather mental states that, given the proper motivation, are ready to enter into action. On this matter, the following quotation from Cervantes is appropriate: "And sir, do not think that I call vulgar only the humble and the commoner, because everyone who is ignorant even though lord or prince can and should be among the ranks of the vulgar" (84, p. 40). Among its objectives, Folklore catalogs and studies these stages so that they can be overcome by education. Unfortunately, because of a lack of scientifically administered programs in this discipline, repressive police actions are many times directed against prelogical individuals.

Back to Educational Folklore

We find it important in Folklore to identify these prelogical mental states in order to make education more effective. Many folkloric activities are not prejudicial to society, while others, the prelogical ones, are a deadly weight preventing the community's progress and should be eliminated. Education, on the other hand, should not act directly against the activity by forcibly preventing it from occurring, but rather it should work on the individual and demonstrate to him that his motivations can be satisfied by different actions and that these may even function more effectively. For example, education teaches that penicillin is more effective than excrement in curing illness. We hope to deal with this large subject in another study.*

*See *Folklore y Educación*, 1st. edition. Quito: Editorial Casa de la Cultura Ecuatoriana, 1961. 315 pp. 2nd edition. Buenos Aires: Editorial Omeba, 1969. 272 pp.

Pioneering Observations of Arthur Ramos

We must note that the great majority of actions characteristic of the prelogical act were observed in Brazil by Arthur Ramos. Although the observations were not explained, they were still one more important contribution to the totality of his scholarly work. Here are some excerpts taken at random from several of his studies: "It is this persistence of the prelogical mentality that explains the survival of fetishist acts among the Negroes of Bahia in our time" (104, p. 295, 406–410). "Folklore is an emotional survival. It is the preservation of prelogical elements which remain in cultures in their struggle to search for their own personality" (103, p. 31). "Folklore is not a simple recreational study. It is a demo-psychological method of analyzing the subconscious of the masses" (103, p. 276). "It is sufficient to peruse any *folklore* study to note the persistence of the survival of the primitive mentality in the thinking process, in actions, in popular institutions, in tales, legends, proverbs, etc." (101, p. 331).

This scholar impresses us with his famous study of the medicasters prepared in 1931 and published and widely distributed in 1937. In it, he states: "In Brazil there are certain places where the continued persistence of the prelogical mentality in medical practices can be verified, especially among those directly under Negro or Indian influence." After mentioning the studies of Nina Rodrigues, his precursor, he adds the following example of a prelogical practice:

The witch doctor asks the client for money, soap, bottles of scent "to prepare the table." He immediately returns one of the pieces of soap and instructs him to take a bath daily for seven days. Meanwhile he asks a fetishist spirit (in this case *Ye-man-já*, the goddess of water) to remove the illness from his body. After the seventh bath the soap must be thrown in the water while the patient recites the following formula:

Viva a Rainha do mar, ina-ê!	Long live the Queen of the sea— She is that!
Princesa do aiocá,* ina-ê . . .	Princess of the *aiocá*—she is that!
Oi-á, oi-á, D. Janaína,	*Oi-á, oi-á,* D. Janaína

*"Aiocá," "ina-ê," "oi-á," "mariê-ê" are currently purely sounds, which formerly probably had meanings in Brazilian-African languages.

Oi-á, oi-á, princesa do mar	*Oi-á, oi-á,* princess of the sea.
oiá mariê-ê	*Oi-á,* she is Maria.
sou de jau-á	I come from an Amazon fish
A onda vai, a onda vem	The waves come and the waves go
Ande brincar, rainha do mar.	Go and play, queen of the sea.

The prelogical mentality governs all medicaster practices of those under the influence of Negro and Indian primitive religions. . . . It can be noted that the problem of folk medicine cannot be solved as easily as it seems. Its curtailment is not merely a matter for the penal code. It implies a slow and persistent educational effort in the area, an effort to develop a more advanced kind of mentality to change the prelogical and mystical elements into logical or rational elements [Lévy-Bruhl] or to change their autistic way of thinking [Eugen Bleuler]. Here Ramos quotes from Bleuler: Neither laws nor insults will effectively combat *curandeiros,** but rather they must be placed on a higher level not only by training their minds but in psychological understanding. . . . Finally, the charlatan must be pursued by the authorities in compliance with the penal code. The *curandeiro,* the last representative of the medicine man, of the shaman, the witch doctor must deserve our careful attention. He must be opposed by educational measures which are reflected in the very areas where he operates. It is a decisive battle between culture and superstition, between the correct and rational and mystical lies and fetishist abuses.

[Further on, Ramos again repeats more insistently and in other words the same theme:] I) A fundamental difference between charlatanism and medicastering must be established as a premise for different attitudes in facing these two phenomena. II) The charlatan is a conscious violator of laws made by social class and must pay the penalties provided by the law. The curandero is an involuntary charlatan whose conduct obeys very different psychological determinents. III) These motives are the prelogical factors of primitive mentality as we find them in the medicine man in primitive societies. The persistence of this mentality in the curandero of our times is very evident in certain areas of Brazil that were directly under Negro or Indian influence. IV) A precise psychological understanding of the phenomena of medicastering is essential to the establishment of correct norms of conduct for those who have followed these practices. V) Repression of medicasters is the slow problem of educating the area where they operate, and of placing correct norms of thinking and rational logic in opposition to their mystical, prelogical and undisciplined practices (102, pp. 74–77).

---

*Curandeiros: The urban folk medicine-men.

These outstanding and clarifying excerpts from this scholar on the prelogical quality of the folkloric act and the ways to combat it, which appeared like a flash in his study, have led us to prepare a study on *Folklore and Education.*

THE FOLKLORIC ACT

Synthesis of General Characteristics of the Folkloric Act

Let us synthesize the general characteristics of the folklore act. As the introduction to this work stated, the folkloric act is a cultural activity of any people that is typified by being anonymous, noninstitutionalized, and eventually by being ancient, functional, and prelogical. Because of its cultural state, we understand its human quality, be that material, immaterial, or social. It is a contrary state to race, constitutions, and civilization. Because of its anonymous quality, it must be conceived as the product of no one single individual, although someone, in theory, was its originator. In spite of this, we avoid confusing the originator with the person who performs the act, that is, the transmitter. The act generally ceases to be folkloric if the transmitter knows the real originator of the act. It becomes folkloric, however, if only scholars know the truth about it. By its noninstitutionalized state, we mean its manner of transmittal. There is only one way in which an act becomes folklorically traditionalized and that is in a noninstitutionalized way. That means that it is neither organized, directed, nor gradual; in other words, it is neither official, heirarchically religious, nor aristocratic. By ancient, we mean the existential age of the act, even though this is a subjective matter and is a problem that still needs to be resolved. By functional condition, we refer to its constant vitality. We understand that the act only exists because it fulfills a role in the society that produced and adopted it. It is like a plant that either grows or dies according to environmental conditions and the attention given it. This attention in turn is limited by motivation. Acts that disappear are acts that lose their function.

Such acts make up the "archeology" of folklore. Although essential for the study of the past, they are only complementarily useful for the study of present-day man. Many call them "dead folklore," a label they prefer to "fossils of folklore." In addition to those authors cited in chapter 4 see, for example, the following: 93, p. 662, 83, pp. 253–254. And, finally, by its prelogical condition, we mean its irrationality, its affective blindness, its faith, the tenacious negativeness of the individual to heed the axiom that urges one to not make the same mistake twice, *non bis in idem*.

By conceptualizing the folkloric act in this way, we exposed our ideas and in so doing symbolized them in words. We are willing to change our ideas and especially our words as this science evolves. We can do so with difficulty, however, if the study of Folklore in the Americas continues without nomenclature. We are compelled, therefore, to standardize a basic nomenclature and to propose a universal minimum list of terms. Only when this has been accomplished will it be possible to discuss ideas and concepts with precision. If at this time everyone continues adopting strange terms, when they are not inventing new ones, it will never be possible to attain concrete objectives. See O. K. Ogden and I. A. Richards' study of *The Meaning of Meaning* (88). Ralph Steele Boggs is another who protests against what he calls terminologists, and the ill of uncontrolled invention of terminology in excess of the true needs of the science (19).

The reader can readily understand the situation by consulting various Folklore manuals. He will note that many authors give the word "civilization" the meaning of "culture," and by "tradition" they mean "antiquity." They label "prelogical" what is "popular" when they do not wish to use "popular" in its political sense, as do the Soviets (112, pp. 5–6). The confusion in concepts and terminology is such that in Portugal the very word "folklore" is substitutable by "ethnography" (39).

Need for a Dictionary of Folklore Theory

To achieve uniformity of basic nomenclature, we propose developing a dictionary of Folklore. This should be a study that explains the terminology of the discipline and the ways in which scholars use it. In fact, such a study would be a dictionary of the chaos of Folklore in our time.*

---

*It is worth noting that I wrote these words in 1956. In 1960, *General Ethnological Concepts* by Ake Hultkrantz was published in Denmark (Copenhagen: Rosenkilde and Bagger, 1960. 282 pp) . This book, among the anthropological dictionaries published until now, is the most valuable for general folklore concepts.

If no one can agree on the components, it is correspondingly more difficult for the total discipline. The state of the concept of folklore is pandemonium. I will never forget Fernando Ortiz, a venerable scholar of Folklore who, at the closing ceremony of the International Congress of Folklore in São Paulo in 1954, stated that for over half a century he had been studying "something that no one knew exactly how to define: folklore" (90, p. 12).

9

Folklore as a Science

As we indicated in our opening remarks, the second and last step of our attempt to conceptualize Folklore concerns its boundaries. Folklore, a branch of cultural anthropology, is the scientific study of the cultural acts of any people. Until now we have been discussing folklore (acts); from here on we will study Folklore (the discipline). We have drawn these boundaries in the ascending order of a pyramid, that is from the general to the particular. In the first place, we will attempt to discover if Folklore belongs to the so-called functions of the spirit or to the power of reason, if it is a subjective or an objective activity. In the second place, if it is an activity of the power of reason and, therefore, a science, we will try to decide what kind of a science it is. Finally, in the third place, we will investigate to determine if Folklore, as a science of cultural man, is or is not related to the other sciences dealing with cultural man. The latter problem deals specifically with the study of the relationships of Folklore, specifically the relation of Folklore to ethnography. In any case, we shall deal with these relationships here because they imply questions of boundaries.

CHARACTERISTICS OF SCIENCE

Folklore is a science because its research can only be accomplished by following the steps that characterize scientific research in general: observation, compilation, criticism, classification, and interpretation. Any study that alters this procedural sequence ceases to be a science and becomes subjective. Scientifically speaking, then, it is never possible to interpret before first observing, compiling, criticizing, and classifying data. A priori interpretations are not interpretations but hypotheses for study. Only an idea provable by facts can be called an interpretation. We will not discuss here all of the steps of the science and technique of Folklore that we must use, although I did so in the first edition of *Concepto de Folklore*. I will limit myself, then, to discussing only some complementary considerations.

Interdependence of the Phases of Research

There is absolute interdependence between the previously mentioned phases, and the scientific value of the research suffers when such interdependence is overlooked. To be scientific presupposes knowing a complete procedure. An individual is not scientific who knows how to observe but not how to compile, or who knows how to compile but not how to classify or criticize. These first four phases are essential for the descriptive folklorist, that is, the ethnographer of folklore. The interpreter performs the fourth phase of the research. He is called a "folklorologist," or an "ethnologist of folklore."* A folklorologist can work with his own data or that of others. He ceases being scientific, and, consequently, his folklore observations are not scientific if the first four phases of the research have not been duly accomplished. On the other hand, even when he has faithfully performed the first four phases of research (observation, compilation, criticism, and classification) the scientific success of the folklorist still depends on his purely interpretative activities. In conclusion, we can apply Costa Pinto's comments about sociology to Folklore: It is possible to study social phenomena scientifically because in social life, in spite of the *sui generis* nature of the phenomena which occur in it, there is a certain order of observable events that no other science studies from the same point of view. There are a certain number of constant and objective relationships among such events, around which relationships research can be realized and hypotheses developed. These hypotheses may or may not be confirmed when contrasted with the facts. In this way, we obtain a sufficient basis for generalizations and

---

*"Folklorologist" instead of "folklorist." In Spanish: "folklorólogo" instead of "folklorista." Also note "ethnologist" vs. "ethnographer."

principles, and from them we can achieve the foresight that characterizes any scientific effort. Science begins or begins again with *criticism*. New mental attitudes and new hypotheses develop from criticism. These must lead to fundamental research that confirms or denies the hypotheses. New objective bases for generalizations and laws are developed by the multiplication and systemizing of the results of research. Arranging these in an organic entity makes or refines science, as it constantly changes (38).

Importance of Each Phase of Research

All the steps in the research process are not only completely interdependent but equally important. We disagree with Albert Marinus, the Belgian scholar, who states tacitly that Folklore does not have the right to label itself a science while it does not attempt to "separate the nexus which tie all the phenomena to each other," that is, until it is cataloged. In his opinion, the individual is only "truly scientific" who "generalizes" and "exerts himself to find the nexus of actions." This means that the person who does not have the aptitude to interpret or is simply not inclined to interpretive tasks but prefers to store and collect thousands upon thousands of acts is not "truly scientific." He is not worth being noticed by Marinus. To reinforce his position, he quotes a paragraph from Pierre Delbet which, it seems to us, is full of mistakes: "There is nothing scientific about a collection of acts even though they are comprehensively observed. A herbarium is not botany, a museum is not zoology, a library catalog is not science. . . . The true scientist is the one who discovers the constant nexus which relate phenomena to each other" (78, p. 8).

Science, on the contrary, develops for us in units that are not distributed by the order of their importance, but rather by need and choice like the steps of a stairway. All of the steps, not just the one at the top, make up a stairway. And it is sufficient for one of them to be weak for the entire structure to collapse or, at best, to prevent our reaching the top. We consider Delbet's example of the herbarium to be a part of the science of botany, and the museum to be a part of the biological sciences. Fundamentally, the stair steps equate with scientific classification. Preceding them are observation, compilation, and criticism, and beyond them, interpretation.

The person who observes, compiles, criticizes, and classifies is as scientific as the one who interprets, generalizes, discovers analogies, and states laws. Without the means, there would be no end.

Reactions of the General Public

One of our greatest hopes is to have the general public consider American folklore as a science. Furthermore, we must prepare for what will happen with the publication in Uruguay of the first monograph in the field.* Its completely descriptive character will cause laughter, disdain, and jeers. This has already occurred in other countries. The readers will wonder how a scholar can spend time with such foolishness. It will be considered useless, inconsequential, and inferior. Nevertheless, the same thing happened when the natural sciences were becoming scientific. Marinus states:

> In Descartes' time there was the same prejudice toward the natural sciences. It was thought that nothing would ever come from the collector's observations of insects, butterflies, shells, birds, mushrooms, plants, flowers, etc. Obviously, Buffon was nothing more than a literary man, and Cuvier but a classifier. And yet their first essays synthesizing and functionally analyzing the problems of life were vigorously attacked. The work of naturalists was considered a repertoire of activities that could not possibly be verified. Nevertheless, Bacon was the first at the beginning of the seventeenth century to battle this "hypothesis of impossibility" (78, pp. 22–23).

And I am certain that more confidence in the scientific studies of folklorists will soon develop. The importance they deserve is already recognized in many countries. This final message of Marinus is true and encouraging, and we should remember it. "We predict that this science [Folklore] will have a future replete with important discoveries. Their effect on the sciences of man will be such that all our current concepts will be overturned" (78, p. 23).

FOLKLORE, AN INDEPENDENT SCIENCE OR NOT

Evolution of the Concept of Anthropology

To ascertain Folklore's place among the sciences precisely, it

*Translator's Note: The first Spanish edition of *The Concept of Folklore* was published in Uruguay in 1956. At that time, the author was preparing the first

is necessary to survey the evolution of the concept of anthropology. We can do so by using Arthur Ramos' synthesis presented in his *Introdução à antropologia brasileira* (100). Three points of view preceded the present concept of anthropology.

Originally, anthropology was synonymous with psychology. Magnus Hunt, in 1501, saw it as the description of the body and the soul and the rules of governing their union. The humanists of the Renaissance, the encyclopedists, and Kant himself, in addition to Magnus Hunt, used the term "anthropology" with the same meaning. Following Kant, Hegel, among the idealists, scarcely modified its meaning when he used it in the title of a chapter in his *Philosophy of the Soul*. Hegelian anthropology, then, was far from what it now hopes to be. It was "the study of the soul as a natural soul, as a sensitive soul or feeling soul, and of the real soul" (57).

In the same century, the anatomists changed the meaning of anthropology. It was accepted as the equal of comparative human anatomy and physiology. In other words, it ceased being the "science of the soul" which it had been and became "a natural science of man examined in his racial milieu." It carries this meaning even today. Actually, only physical anthropology is restricted to this meaning. The term "anthropology" by itself has acquired a much broader meaning: the study of man not only examined in his racial environment but in his cultural environment as well.

Like the anatomists who incorporated the human racial setting in anthropology, geographers and historians incorporated the cultural dimension. They called their studies "ethnography," a term created by Camper in 1807. It deals with the branch of history or geography responsible for the description of primitive people of the world. In time, this definition was extended to include any people, primitive or not. In 1839, ethnography was enriched by the notion of ethnology in which one can state laws on ethnical studies.

Obviously, ethnography and ethnology were not able to remain branches of history and geography for long. As soon as they were created, there were disagreements on purposes and objectives, even though all four disciplines employed the so-called historical-

Uruguayan monograph in the field, as a group project: *Folklore floridense. Contribución.* Lima, Perú: Reprint of *Folklore Americano*, Año V, N.5, 1957, pp. 5–60.

cultural method. Finally, a complete separation took place. Cultural anthropology and physical anthropology joined under the general label, anthropology, the science of man.

Folklore as a Part of Cultural Anthropology

With the passing of time, both branches of anthropology were subdivided, the physical into, among others, paleontology, physical archeology, biotypology. The cultural was subdivided into such sciences as paleoethnology, cultural archeology, ethnography, ethnology, linguistics, and Folklore. Arguments concerning the dependence or independence of these disciplines fill the pages of many treaties. I see no point in taking a side on this issue. Nothing is substantially changed if it is stated that Folklore is or is not independent. It seems logical to me, however, to recognize it as a part of cultural anthropology. Among others, Alfredo Nutt, E. Sidney Hartland, and Stanislad Wake want it this way (84, p. 28), as do Arthur Ramos and Imbelloni in the Americas. Defining Folklore, Ramos emphasized: "Folklore is the branch of cultural anthropology which studies those aspects of the culture of any people relating to traditional literature" (96). Imbelloni, on the other hand, defines it as: "That division of cultural anthropology which deals with traditional lore of the masses of civilized nations" (62, p. 37).

The Differences Between Folklore and Ethnography

The relationship between Folklore, ethnography, and ethnology involves the question of boundaries. They are all three so interrelated that at certain levels there are conflicting opinions as to where one ends and another begins. Because we consider Folklore as studying the actions of any people, how then can we distinguish between them? There are three arguments in play here: (1) The argument concerning the characteristics of the folkloric act. (2) The argument concerning plebeian or folk survivances among civilized people. (3) The argument concerning ethnographic exclusiveness of cultural material.

The only way we can differentiate clearly between Folklore and ethnography is to define the characteristics of the folkloric act. We repeat, the folkloric act is cultural, belongs to any people, and its principal characteristics are that it is anonymous and not institutionalized, and eventually old, functional, and prelogical. On the other hand, the ethnographic act is also cultural, belongs to any people, is also functional, and may be old and prelogical. It is not, however, anonymous, nor is it noninstitutionalized. Were it to adopt these characteristics, it would be folkloric. Folklore does not study culture as a whole but rather a specific type of cultural act. It is advisable when analyzing an area to avoid breaking up its cultural unity with boundaries between folkloric acts and ethnographic acts. I am inclined to praise the Portuguese for having simplified the question by using the term "ethnography." Folklore is ethnography and ethnography is folklore as far as they are concerned. This action, however, is absurd for the exacting scholar.

The second argument reminds us of the attitude of the New World's first geographers and historians toward what they called the "savage," or "primitive." As a term, "ethnography" was developed in 1807 to identify the studies of these same savage or primitive people. "Folklore" as a term was developed in 1846 to mean studies of culture, not of savages or primitive men but rather of their equivalents among civilized groups. This is not a simple position like that of the Portuguese but a simplistic one, and, consequently, we must reject it. The two disciplines differ then not by the object studied by each but by the bearer of that object. The same item, material or not, found in the possession of indigenous people was ethnography but it became folklore if found in the possession of peasants or laborers. To speak of "Indian folklore" was something unusual. It is evident that we are dealing with a frankly European discussion that is perhaps valid in the Old World where the cultural features of the peasants and workers are very different from those of indigenous cultures. In America, however, where we have inherited Indian customs extensively, this difference is nothing more than a rather captious sophism. Incredibly, however, the 1954 International Folklore Congress in São Paulo approved the European formula that the universe of Folklore is located in the plebeian strata of civilized societies. We fought courageously to the very end of the meeting against the European block of that Congress who were jealous of their prerogatives as precursors of Folklore. They gave abundant proof, with their excellent culturocentric ideas concerning us, of their proverbial ignorance of the problems of the New World.

The third argument has fortunately been overcome. They wanted Folklore to be the study of nonmaterial cultural manifestations because the material ones were part of ethnography. In other words, ideational-verbal culture (verses, myths, legends, tales) was folklore, while the motor-perceptive culture was ethnography. Only small groups of scholars think this way today.

The Problem of "Indian folklore"

Naturally, each one of these arguments has a brief of opinions for or against it. To gather them is to write the history of Folklore. Merely as an illustration, I will review the principal opinions on the problem of Indian folklore that either support or refute the argument concerning plebeian survivances in civilized people. Let us begin with the Boggs-Jacovella polemic that started in the *Revista del Instituto Nacional de la Tradición* in Buenos Aires (20). Boggs supported the recognition of "primitive" folklore while Jacovella, supported by Jijena Sánchez, refuted this position in another article (65). Boggs' thesis insisted on the fact that it would be absurd to prepare thematic monographs excluding the Indian's contribution, especially when the discovery of a universal folklore theme is imminent. He writes that it would be absurd to study all the variants of the great flood theme in world folklore (as Frazer does in his *Folklore in the Old Testament*, chapter IV, for approximately 250 pages, bringing together variants from ancient Babylon, the Maori of New Zealand, from Peru, the Carajá of Brazil, etc.) and on discovering variants found among primitive people, fail to take them into account and state that the primitive cannot be considered as folklore (20). Supporting his position, he cites scholars who, in extensive studies, included acts of primitive people, as well as the theoretical works of others who openly advocated their inclusion. In support of his position, Jacovella refuted Boggs by declaring that folklore does not exist when the Indian group has only one culture. On the other hand, if the Indian group has a "folk culture" side by side with a learned culture, then the folk culture may contain folkloric elements. He says:

> Some indigenous people of the American continent pose a difficult problem concerning this. Which discipline will study them, ethnography or folklore? Our reply is consistent. If they live at the edge

of mestizo masses together with their chiefs, language, religion, customs, and techniques, without any contamination from the former or with only isolated borrowings that do not change their general way of life, their study falls in the realm of ethnography. On the other hand, if they share the general patterns of mestizo life, fall under its political and civil system, speak the national language even though preserving the indigenous one, practicing and respecting either faithfully or imperfectly the Catholic religion, and practicing mestizo and indigenous customs and techniques, in sum, living like a social substratum next to the mestizo folk, as occurs for example with the remains of the Incanato, then it is just to assign the study of them to folklorists (20, p. 37).

Both Boggs and Jacovella cite scholars supporting and opposing the inclusion of the "primitive" in Folklore. The former cites among others, H. Callaway who in 1868 published his children's tales of the Zulus; George McCall's *Kafir Folklore* published in 1886; Frazer's *Golden Bough* (whose first edition was published in 1890 in which the author did not omit citing the parallels from Africa or any other primitive people which happened to interest him); the *Memorials* of the American Folklore Society which in 1894 presented "A Collection of 50 traditional tales from Angola with texts in Ki-mbundu and English translations"; George Lawrence Gomme who, in 1890, defined Folklore and stated that "a great deal of the folklorist's material must be obtained from . . . savage and primitive people"; Anti Aarne, who, in 1914, included collections from the "primitives" of Africa in his *Uebersicht der Märchenliteratur,* and Walter Anderson, who, in 1923, in his comparative study of the traditional tale "The Emperor and the Abbot," discloses no less than 474 variants in which some of the "primitives" take part. Supporting his position, Bruno Jacovella cites the *California Folklore Quarterly* which, in 1942, stated that the California Folklore Society's objectives were the collection, preservation, and publication of folk materials of the state of California and adjacent regions, excluding those belonging to indigenous tribes, their mythology and ethnology. Specifically included in the California Folklore Society are tales and songs, customs and superstitions, proverbs and epigrams, place names, local patterns of architecture, furniture, and implements of all racial groups (except the North American Indian) which join to make up the *folk* of the area of the Pacific slope. In this study, Jacovella cites no other

sources, nor does he criticize any of those mentioned by Boggs with
the exception of Frazer's book. Concerning *The Golden Bough*,
Jacovella denies its folkloric exclusivism and suggests, as does
Jijena Sánchez later, that it is an "extensive ethnological monograph" (65, p. 225).

Wilhelm Schmidt, in his *Manuale di Metodologia Etnologica*,
writes in Germany that "restricting folklore to the culture of
nations whose race is white as A. Haberland wishes *(Die deutsche
Volkskunde*, Halle an der Saale, 1935, p. 150) cannot even be
supported" (110, p. 268).

Ismael Moya in Argentina contends that "it is a mistake to omit
the area of traditional Indian customs from a folkloric study on
the basis of its encroaching on the field of ethnography. A large
number of these customs remained among those kept up by the
Creoles, although they have softened them and modified them to
a modern context. Following the trail of a present-day plebeian
habit can lead one to a remote indigenous practice" (84, p. 168).
Later Moya states again, "In my opinion it is a mistake to deny
Indian myths folkloric validity on the basis that they are included
in the study of ethnography" (84, p. 185).

Melville Herskovits in North America, after materially restricting the boundaries of Folklore, increases them with reference to the
"primitive." He believes that folklore, in the sense of plebeian
literature, is not limited to cultures without writing systems, nor
to defined levels of "civilized" societies, since it is universal in
human civilization. Folklore must, consequently, be treated equally
to any other aspect of culture. It is based on this criterion that
Herskovits uses the examples of Boas collected in *Mythology and
Folk-tales of the North American Indians* and judges Boas' book a
tour de force of folkloric analysis that was never again equaled (58).

Daniel Ortega Ricaurte of Colombia is the author of an article
on "Indigenous Folklore in America" (89). Gustavo Barroso in
Brazil translated to French his *Mythes, contes et légendes des
indiens* and gave it the subtitle *Folk-Lore Brésilien* (14). And Câmara Cascudo discusses the topic in two pages of his monumental
Literatura Oral. He feels that there are no people who possess one
culture alone, which is reminiscent of Paul Saintyves' statement,
"Folklore studies plebeian life, but within civilized life." Câmara
Cascudo concludes, "Thus I believe there are indigenous and

Negro folklores . . ." (23, pp. 27, 28). Renato Almeida also concedes the existence of Indian folklore, acclaiming it in his *Inteligência do Folklore*, a study subsequent to the first edition of our *Concepto*. He writes: "And as a result of what is evident and known, I define Folklore as the combination of noninstitutionalized manifestations of the spiritual life and of the forms of material culture flowing from or associated with it in primitive peoples or in the plebeian classes of civilized societies" (3, p. 41).

According to Javier Guerrero, in 1936 Professor Basauri published *La Psicología del Indio a través de su Folklore* in a newspaper article in Mexico (56, p. 100). In addition to the CEAP in Paraguay, Anselmo Jover Peralta, the linguist, also accepts a folklore of the Indian. He writes, "The Guaraní Indians never experienced writing. Their entire literature, consisting primarily of tales, poems, orations, myths, narratives, and legends, is oral and folkloric" (68, p. XV).

Among the Americans opposing the adherents of Indian folklore is George Herzog who, in his study *Research on Primitive and Folkloric Music in the United States*, emphasizes a quite sharp separation (59).

Imbelloni, in Argentina, contends that during the period of inquiry,

> It is in no way advisable to continue confusing the compilation of the ceremonies that are peculiar to native people in general with those that make up the substratum of civilized nations. We know well that we will frequently find vestiges and elements of something in the substratum of our people which can only be explained by examining the comparisons of these native groups. Nevertheless, this does not constitute a justification for Folklore journals to dedicate themselves *ex-profeso* to the Hottentots, the Polynesians, and the Red Skins, to take and describe their songs, rituals, and fables. . . . If we wish to follow a less reprehensible line, we must classify the myths of the Ojibwa, Sauk, Sioux, Chippewa, etc., as ethnographic research because they do not, in any way, stand for an underlying *substratum* of North American culture, but rather the very culture of local tribes artificially preserved. With reference to myths, ceremonies, and songs of Peru and Bolivia on the other hand, many aboriginal elements survive and are related to the national culture under the guise of substrata. Their integral separation from the folkloric whole becomes not only cumbersome if not often improper (62, pp. 89–90).

Saintyves, in addition to defining the area of folkloric study, went on to state that there is no folklore in people where two cultures cannot be distinguished, that of the learned class and that of the masses. It is necessary for the definition of folklore to specify that it deals with plebeian knowledge and behavior in civilized people. There is a folklore of the majority of the people of India or China but there is no Kafir or Peu folklore. Among the latter, national behavior belongs entirely in the realm of ethnography (23, p. 27).

In 1923, Raffaele Corso felt that "Folklore only exists in civilized people. The ways, techniques, practices, beliefs, and artistic production of uncivilized people belong to ethnography" (67, p. 14). Both Jijena Sánchez and Jacovella believed that in Corso's definition, this matter was explained formally for the first time (67, p. 13). They restated their belief later in 1942, 1948, and 1950 (66; Jacovella in 20, pp. 35–38; 65).

Twenty-eight years after his statement, in 1951, Corso changed his view completely, which is laudable in a scholar of his standing. He wrote an article for this purpose titled, "The New Idea of Folklore," in which he disowned his former point of view and praised "American folklorists," who "think in part, that folklore is not a collection of survivances but rather a living scientific mass that embraces in the first place Indians and Negroes" (33, p. 84). Corso reaches the conclusion that "it can be said that the inquiry that reduced folklore to the traditional manifestations of common people or plebeians was overcome, since folklorists are now agreed that the duty of their research is tradition, wherever it is exhibited or appears. . . ." I ask if Jacovella and Jijena who followed Corso so assiduously will not change due to this magnificent apostasy? Unfortunately, it does not appear so, since in January 1951, the same month in which the published Spanish version of the Italian theoretician's revision appeared, the Argentine Ministry of Education distributed a *Manual-Guía para el recolector de folklore* in which Jacovella, its author, states,

> The culture of communities inhabited by aborigenes who live along the edge of civilized society with their own language, religion, customs, and institutions does not fall in the realm of folklore. Their study belongs to ethnography. American folkloric research does not include, then, the culture of indigenous groups unless the latter are assimiliated in Creole or civilized society and

make up a part of its substratum sharing its language, religion, customs and subject to its institutions as occurs in many places in Hispanic America (64, p. 2). [In an annotation apart he continues] It is worth noting that the majority of Anglo-Saxon folklorists and ethnographers label all oral culture (poems, tales, legends, etc.) *Folklore,* and only that, whenever it is found in either uncivilized communities, or in the substrata of civilized societies. On the other hand, the remainder of the world's folklorists study the entire culture of the (civilized) substratum, and ethnography the entire culture of uncivilized groups. This is the position adopted in Argentina.

Chronology of a Polemic

In order to state the chronology of this polemic precisely, let us review the following outline:

1923. Corso wrote *II Folklore* in which he stated, "The customs, techniques, practices, beliefs and artistic production of uncivilized peoples belong to ethnology" (67, p. 14).

1939. Jijena Sánchez and Jacovella published *Las Supersticiones* in which they defended the position of the "eminent Italian folklorist Raffaele Corso" (67, p. 13).

1942. While editing *Instrucciones generales para la recolección de material folklórico* to be put in practice by the National University of Tucumán, Jijena Sánchez reaffirmed his point of view and stated his concept of Folklore as follows: "In brief, let us state that Folklore is a science whose primary objective is the scientific study of the different cultural and traditional practices of the plebeian classes of civilized society. This is so because the spiritual and material culture of uncivilized people belongs to ethnography, its closest neighboring discipline" (66, p. 6.)

1948. Ralph Steele Boggs in his *Lo primitivo y lo material en el Folklore* restated his original point of view of 1943 in an essay defining folklore published in *Folklore Americas.* Making indirect reference to Jacovella and Jijena Sánchez, he states that some say that folklore only exists in civilized groups where there is a folk or lower class with little or no formal education as contrasted with the educated, erudite, upper or civilized class, whereas in primitive groups there is only one culture which is not folklore (20).

1948. Jacovella felt this statement to be an allusion to his position and answered Boggs immediately with a *Nota de la Redacción* (20, pp. 35–38).

1950. Jijena Sánchez does not remain silent either and the following year, July 14, 1949, he read a paper, published in 1950, in which he discusses and evaluates Boggs' point of view, among others, and states, "The position of Dr. Boggs was eloquently refuted by the editor of the journal himself, and we can do no less than agree with the statements of this editor" (65, pp. 224–225).

1951. In Italy, a more mature Corso changes his ideas and expresses their new orientation in November 1950 in an article translated and published by the Bulletin of the Tucuman Folklore Association for January-February 1951 (33). For what reason did Corso send this article to be disseminated in Argentina in Spanish? It is worth noting that in 1951 in an old study, *Essay on Folkloric Studies in Paraguay* (27), we still denied the possibility that Indian folklore existed. Fortunately, we have now risen above this position.

Basic Arguments Supporting "Indian folklore"

In a final synthesis, let us now review the basic arguments supporting Indian folklore.

1. Indian Folklore must be accepted because, as Boggs points out, sciences are not different because of the subject matter they study but, rather, because of their points of view (20).

2. Folklore's subject matter is cultural acts, primarily anonymous and noninstitutionalized, and additionally ancient, prelogical, and functional. Primitive acts can also possess these characteristics.

3. Finally, an Indian folklore must be recognized since comparative folklore would be meaningless if analogous acts were excluded solely because they were collected from indigenous communities.

10

What Folklore Is Not

FASHION

We have completed the object of this study, the conceptualization of Folklore, but we feel that a few words concerning those acts that are often erroneously classified as folkloric would provide a positive contribution.

Concept

Fashion as an act is characterized as highly collectivized, having a known author, having an institutionalized apprenticeship, being preferentially urban, and being of short duration. As we can see, the majority of these characteristics are completely the opposite of those identifying the folkloric act. How then can we explain their being confused with each other except by the complete scientific ignorance of the common people? A high degree of collectivization is currently called "popularity." One speaks of "popular music," not "folklore music." The former almost always has a known author and is usually disseminated by radio or television, especially in urban areas. It has a short but intense life. It is, as Félix Molina Téllez stated, an act that includes what he calls the "circumstancially popular" as opposed to what Jijena and Jacovella called the "traditionally popular" (81, p. 25; 67, p. 20). Gabriel Tarde, in his famous *Les Lois de l'Imitation* in 1890, made the observation that style is completely contrary to tradition. Uniting the ideas of fashion and novelty, Tarde even observed that imitation is one of the principles govering its transmittal as a result of fear of social control (108, pp. 8, 9).

We must attempt, however, to avoid confusion between a folk-loric act and a popularized act, even if the latter is "completely national," as stated by Oneyda Alvarenga (5, p. 231), or is part of the repertory of the folk music of the urban people (59, p. 415). When dealing with music, the aspect of anonymity must be invoked each time a doubt arises. This factor, together with the others, will effectively help us stake out the limits we must keep constantly in mind in order to separate the folkloric act from the popular and also the folkloric act from aesthetic projections.

Examples

Let us look at some examples. "India"* the *guarania* immortalized by M. Ortiz Guerrero and J. Asunción Flores in Paraguay, as well as "El cachivachero," Rubén Carámbula's Uruguayan *candombe,* and our many *sambas, choros, marchas de carnaval,* and *frevos,*** which have authors whose rights are legally protected, are not folkloric expressions. Folkloric music is, for example, the kind collected by Mário de Andrade, Oneyda Alvarenga, Camargo Guarnieri, Martin Braunwieser, and other in the service of the Public Municipal Record Library of São Paulo. This music was carefully studied and the research, primarily by Oneyda Alvarenga, appears in such important works as: *Melodías registradas por meios não-mecânicos* (10), *Xangô* (43),† *Tambor-de-Mina e Tambor-de-Crioulo* (42), *Catimbó* (41), and *Babassuê* (40).

The wooden votive offerings of the precious collection of the Folkloric Museum of the Public Municipal Record Library of São Paulo (9) in the field of cultural material are folkloric, while the ceramics of the Marzal in Paraguay, and the present-day cloth dolls of Señorita Magdalena de Alcántara of São Paulo that are found in confectioner's shops, bookstores, perfume shops are not. On the other hand, in the genre of oral literature, the previously cited *Martin Fierro* as well as many gaucho tales from official Uruguayan

---

*India. Ortiz Guerrero, M., and Asunción Flores, J. RCA Victor Record. Recorded in Argentina. 60–1627–A Samuel Aguayo and his Great Paraguayan Orchestra. Vocalist: Samuel Aguayo.

**Translator's Note: Brazilian dances.

†*Xangô.* Record FM 12–B. Terreiro of Santa Bárbara, Recife, Pernambuco, 26–II–1938. "Registros Sonoros do Folklore Musical Brasileiro," Public Municipal Record Library. Words and music of the texts in "Xangô," Public Municipal Record Library.

literature, brought together by Domingo A. Caillava (22), are precious examples of "popularized" acts.

THE AESTHETIC PROJECTION

Aesthetic Projection and Fashion

At the outset, it is necessary to explain the difference between aesthetic projection and fashion. Although there may be much in common, not every projection is popularized. There are projections that have limited circulation, that is, they have a limited acceptance, and some are limited to society's intellectual elite. On the other hand, the projection is a deliberate simulation of folklore, an imitation, and this is not the purpose of style or fashion.

Concept of Aesthetic Projection

In conceptualizing aesthetic projection, I would say that it is the demophyletic simulation of folklore, and as such is characterized by a change of transmitters, a change of motivation, a change of function, a change of forms, and a change of learning. I say "demophyletic" in reference to those "defined attitudes toward Folklore," which were outlined by Efraín Morote Best. The noted Peruvian scholar states,

> Demophyles are individuals who find through Folklore a kind of romantic excursion into the past. They do not have a clear concept of this science's objectives although they feel something in it like a return to our own environments, something like a path leading to ourselves. They cherish this science, they are always cordially ready to cooperate with anyone who asks for help in its name, and, at the same time, they are always ready to help the known and the unknown, the probable, the sure, the authentic, and the apocryphal (83, p. 9).

Aesthetic projectors, in our opinion, belong to the category of "demophyles" and should not be confused with counterfeiters who are fully aware of the damage they bring about.

Concerning the remaining characteristics of projection, that is change of transmitters, motivation, function, form, and apprenticeship, the reader already knows what these terms mean. But, as an example, let us take the so-called Creole societies of the Rio de la Plata. The folklore that inspires them and that they wish to reproduce to "save it from extinction," loses its specific function once they adopt it, since the motivation that governs it is now different. It next loses its form since a change of motivation and function almost always equate with a change of form. Furthermore, in these Creole societies, the transmission is institutionalized, not spontaneous. And the transmitter, in turn, is an individual of high social status, and so lacks many characteristics that would identify him as folk, plebeian, or prelogical. Writing later than us, Augusto Raúl Cortazar agrees and states,

> The students of an official school of folkloric dances, or an artistic ensemble of any kind, interpret on stage Creole dances for the recreation of the public. Are these folkloric performances? No, and for several reasons. 1) They are not spontaneously performed by the people. 2) They result from systematic instruction, controlled by principles and objectives that are at times pedagogical or aesthetic and are not the fruit of empirical and free learning. 3) Such dances are not performed as the functional expression of an integrating phenomenon of a geographically circumscribed folkloric conglomerate. 4) The dances and performers did not receive the music and dances as the anonymous legacy of their forefathers, as traditional property that was collectivized in their environment but rather as disciplined instruction administered in a methodical manner. 5) They can be considered as projections or stylizations inspired by folklore in its true sense, and they can not be confused (35, pp. 42–43).

Aesthetic Projection and Education

Aesthetic projection infers the ideas of inspiration and utilization as a result of the action of education on Folklore. When Félix Coluccio, for example, refers to some of the subjects of his biographies, he classifies them as ". . . writers, poets, artists, etc., who exploit the folkloric thematic" (31, p. 89). On another occasion, he states, "without being folklorists exclusively, they exploit folkloric subjects for their artistic and literary creations etc., and for different reasons we should know them" (31, p. 11). Mário de Andrade also uses the same term. Recognizing the existence of these inspirations, he found fault with them for being "a middle-class form of pleasure (pleasant reading, recordings for amusement) that consists exclusively in exploiting the folkloric arts for what they can exhibit that is beautiful to the upper classes" (7, p. 286). CEAP, the Center for Paraguayan Anthropological Studies, used the expression "of folkloric inspiration," and in the exposition that was held during the First Paraguayan Folklore Week, various pieces that were presented were cataloged this way. Let us not think, however, that aesthetic projection is the sole kind of such exploitation. In addition to it, there is what we call "inserted folklore" and "fabricated folklore."* But to define these concepts would not be appropriate here.

Another problem concerned with aesthetic projection versus education is the one dealing with deviant cases of exploitation of rejected folklore. As we know, education divides folklore into what is usable and what has been rejected. By education's definition, what was rejected should not be utilized. Prior to any use, selection must take place. This choice of material for aesthetic projection is based on the characteristics of the acts to be utilized as well as the rejected acts. We find the ethical, the aesthetic, the testable, the imaginative, the mnemonic, the motivational, and the concordant are usable. The genital, the scatological, the para-scatological, the para-psychopathological, and the aggressive are not usable.** In spite of everything, from time to time, acts falling in the latter categories are utilized. Ernesto Morales' book *El niño en las leyendas americanas,* written for educational purposes, is an example of this. Morales, maintaining that it is possible to find themes in American folklore for a contemporary writer to weave original and excellent children's tales, attempted to do so using phantoms, fairies, cannibals, the "pora," the "jaci-jateré,"† and the bogeyman (in 105, p. 2). Félix Real Torralba and Hernando Molinari criticized him in very interesting articles in which they unwittingly defended the present view of educational folklore. Real Torralba states, for example, that in Morales' book there was neither a "moral nor a didactic" objective, and that "these narra-

---

*Translator's Note: In Spanish: "folklore intercalado" and "folklore inventado."

**In the first edition of *Concepto de Folklore,* I had not yet developed this classification of acts that are usable or unusable. In *Folklore y Educacion* these are conceptualized in detail.

†Translator's Note: or *sací-pereré.* In Brazilian folklore, a small one-legged Negro who pesters wayfarers at night, or who sets traps for them.

tives in which everything is absurd, artificial, imaginary, cannot be the modern method of pedagogy to develop the child's intellect" (105, p. 2). Molinari was even more precise, "Ernesto Morales' *sin*, according to my way of thinking, consists in having chosen, as we shall see later, the bad part of the rich aboriginal cultural heritage" (80, p. 2).

Synonyms of Aesthetic Projection

Some synonyms for aesthetic projection are "nativism," *costumbrismo*, and "traditionalism." Jesús C. Romero is among those who prefer costumbrismo. "Folkloric *costumbrismo* is folklore embellished with an artistic objective, turned into literature by an erudite artist who does not create folklore but rather gives it a stylized presentation with extra-folkloric objectives" (109, p. 797). L. C. Barbosa Lessa proposes the term "traditionalism," having written a thesis on its "meaning and value." He states:

> Traditionalism is not confused with Folklore, Literature, Theater, etc. All these constitute *means* for Traditionalism to achieve its ends. Traditionalism, a *movement,* must not be confused with Folklore, History, Sociology, etc. which are sciences. A folklorist, for example, must not be confused with a traditionalist. The former is the student of a science, the latter a soldier in a movement. Traditionalists do not need to treat folklore scientifically. They will be performing efficiently if they utilize as a base of action, the studies of folklorists (12, p. 7).

Personally, we favor the term "aesthetic projection," which was devised by Carlos Vega (122, p. 60). We prefer it because its concept almost infers the meaning of the word itself. It deals, in fact, with a projection of folklore in the erudite fields of art, music, and literature. It is aesthetic because it respects beauty in accordance with elite concepts of beauty.

Examples of Projections

As examples of projections, we can cite the gaucho projection, the Negro projection, and the fake "folklore weeks" to mention only the best known ones in the Americas. The gaucho projections of Uruguay even have social organizations that call themselves "Creole Societies." *La Criolla* of Montevideo, *La Querencia* of Carmelo, *Potros y Palmas* of Las Piedras, *La Criolla Artiguista* also of Las Piedras, *Mi Tapera* of Santa Lucía, and *Tradición Oriental* of Canelones are well known. They are centers for social gatherings and for the institutionalized instruction of music, dances, and songs that project the spirit of the gaucho, who is felt, in a general way, to be the founder of the nation. They are made up of men and women coming from middle classes of society. Strictly speaking, and in spite of their statements to the contrary, they have nothing to do with folklore. There is, of course, no lack of bibliographical material concerning such projections. Domingo A. Caillava, for example, quotes many sources of poetry, tales, and scholarly novels with plebeian inspiration in his *Historia de la Literatura Gauchesca en el Uruguay.* His work is similar to that of John T. Howard's "Composers who have used our Folk Songs", a chapter of his *Our American Music* (59, p. 394) and Henriqueta Rosa Fernandes Braga's *O Cancioneiro Folklórico Infantil e sua contribuição à Música Erudita* (46). Negro projections are a fever that has spread to many lands as Ortiz Oderigo notes in his preface to Blaise Cendrars' *Antología Negra* (30). In the Americas, we find these projections in books of Negro "folklore." These books generally contain stereotyped sketches of Negroes and much onomatopoeic poetry. The so-called "folklore weeks" are worse. They bring together the gaucho and the Negro, symphonic orchestras, dance troops from the municipal theater, and reciters. These are weeks that are public successes and anything but the success of study committees pledged to discuss theses and plans concerning research techniques, models for classification, results of comparisons, methods of interpretation, and complete folkloric record of the republic.

Protests of Folklore Scholar

Folklorists naturally do not sit still before such abuse. There are already many protests against "contrived folklore"* and against projections that use the term. Let us note Mário de Andrade for example,

There is yet another plague. I do not know if it is universal or not, but it set out among us to prejudice Folklore. In addition to the indifference of governments and millionaires, scientific folklore in

---

*Contrived folklore: fabricated folklore. In Spanish: "folklore inventado."

Brazil puts up with the shameless competition of the hobbyists, which is scandalously protected by publishing houses and public acclaim. One example to illustrate this confusion is sufficient. It is a general practice among extemporaneous singers on the radio, records, and even concerts to call themselves "folkloric" merely because they use and abuse songs of the people, changing the words, and modifying their melodies to achieve "greater vocal facility," I have been told, and completely deforming their instrumentation and harmony. And not only that but certain anthologists of songs and popular anecdotes who are ignorant but of unquestioned good will are unanimously accepted as folklorists not only in advertisements and by managers, but by the educated public and newspaper critics as well. . . . Truly this "folklore" which makes up books and magazines, or songs on radio or records, anecdotes, peculiar customs, traditional music, and poems of the people resembles primarily a process of achieving social supremacy by the middle class. It is still not the search for knowledge, the usefulness of a legitimate interpretation, nor a desire for human sympathy (7, pp. 285–286) .

Arthur Ramos also protests indignantly,

Folklore in Brazil is a more or less depraved term. I have already shown on more than one occasion the tragic fate of certain expressions having a legitimate scientific origin and which fell into total discredit among us. . . . In Brazil, Folklore became converted to songs on the radio. Any radio star at all is introduced as a "distinguished interpreter of our folklore." The popular composer becomes a folklorist. The popular musical program is "an hour dedicated to our folk-lore." . . . The distinguished virtuoso traveling with his instrument in distant lands, singing things about Brazil—which are very interesting without any doubt—is considered nothing more or less than "a specialist emeritus of our folklore." Radio commentators, literary critics, radio announcers . . . daily speak of Folklore and refer to skillful qualities of the previously mentioned "folklorists." . . . One of our most valued musicians, who comes close to being a genius, considers himself one of the greatest specialists on "folklore," as if "folklore" was compatible with individual creativity or could undergo deformation by the subjective factor! "Folklore" is a scientific discipline. It has nothing to do with these deformed creations. Its examination is objective since common property is being dealt with, and its patrimony is a collective patrimony (95, pp. 227, 228).

Additional protests were heard during the Brazilian Folklore Con-

gress of 1951. Raúl Lima hoped, for example, that the holding of
the First Brazilian Folklore Congress would serve as an opportunity
to initiate a campaign of honesty and good taste against the deformation undergone by folklore which has converted it into a type
of vaudeville on the radio and in the theater and that there is
nothing sadder nor any more intolerable than the deformation of
something so serious, beautiful, and important as the reproduction
of customs and traditional manifestations of the traditional art
of the people. He notes than an unfortunate confusion begins to
exist between folklore and the real or doubtful talents of any
"bum" at all who goes about interpreting the types of poor rural
people. He adds that it behooves true scholars and those interested
in Folklore to organize themselves against these charlatans and
detractors (74 pp. 199–200).

Undoubtedly, the congresses and protests in Brazil diminish
the prestige of erroneous aesthetic projections. It was possible to
show many people that these projections were not in defense of
what is ours, that is, what is national, as maintained by many of
the projectors. National things can only be safeguarded if they
are scientifically collected in museums and in technical monographs, not by imitations developed for the "love of homeland"
that do not have, nor should they have, any other objective than
to be a social or intellectual diversion.

Measures to be adopted

Considering what scholars have stated, certain measures should
be adopted that would satisfy folklorists' reasons and satisfy the
emotional anxiety of the aesthetic inspirers. For want of others, I
propose the following guidelines: (1) That aesthetic projectors
(poets, literary personalities, musicians, and such people) take their
place as aesthetic projectors and stop considering themselves as
"preservers." They preserve nothing. Their activities are nothing
more than social amusements, subjective productions, nostalgic
national exteriorizations that demonstrate love for the acts of the
people, but little understanding of these acts. This, because scientifically speaking, they do not collect, they do not classify, they do
not compare, they do not interpret. They scarcely do more than
imitate. (2) That any exploitation based on materials already in-
vestigated and published should specify its source. Paul Sébillot's

lesson on this topic is magnificent. On composing *La Bretagne Enchantée,* he advised in the subtitle that it dealt with "poetry on popular themes." He states, "Poets do not ordinarily indicate the sources that inspired them. I felt that in this volume, composed solely of pieces each of which originates from a popular theme, that I should acknowledge the material I used" (111, p. 271). (3) Under no circumstances should they call themselves folklorists or folklorologists because they do not deal with folklore. They are "traditionalists," *costumbristas,* "nativists," "aesthetic projectors," and "interpreters." Raúl Lima in his protest emphasized the need for defending "folklore" as a term as well as a concept. Lima writes,

> The National Folklore Commission, a branch of the IBECC, should be vigilant of the word identifying its activities with the same determination as the Red Cross struggles for the exclusive use of its internationally honored and respected emblem. We need to develop a system for the cultural protection of the word whose centennial commemoration occurred some time ago. The National Folklore Commission must keep vigilant and whenever this rich word is used ostensively and unwarrantedly, combat it, denounce it, or at least show its disapproval or expressly deny the propriety of such use. As we know, the false "typical," the so-called "regional," presenting grotesque and sordid caricatures of our people from the interior, is now being called "folklore," and this is definitely corruption and adulteration and justifies the reaction of those developing a defamed science (74, p. 200).

(4) In each city of each country where graduates of regular Folklore courses reside, study centers should be established whose objective is to research, publish, develop new courses and lectures, and organize congresses. Hopefully as a natural process, more light will be shed and the projections will be obliged to follow an appropriate path.

11

A Schematic Diagram

One of the complementary problems of Folklore is that of ascertaining the place of the "Concept of Folklore" among the folkloric disciplines. To state this precisely, I must use a schematic diagram because of the dimension and complexity of folkloric science. I am certain the intelligent reader will not miss the related explanations and will be able to find his way unassisted. He must also understand that not all aspects of folklore will be listed here since this diagram is nothing more than a guide.

0.0 FOLKLORIC SCIENCE

0.1 *General Folklore.* A group of theories and doctrines that define folklore as one of the branches of human knowledge.

0.2 *Regional Folklore.* Studies effected by the use of the rudiments of general Folklore on geographical entities. These are community studies such as Folklore of Ecuador, Folklore of Brazil, Folklore of the United States.

0.3 *Comparative Folklore.* They are parallels of regional folklore.

0.4 *Applied Folklore.* Studies of folkloric acts according to the norms of education, that is to say, analysis of the acts of an area that should be protected and restored and those that should be tracked down and eliminated.

0.1 GENERAL FOLKLORE

1.1 Concept of Folklore ⎤
1.2 Field Folklore   ⎬ Basic Course
1.3 Factual Folklore   ⎦

1.4   Interdisciplinary Folklore ⎫
1.5   History of Folklore   ⎬ Advanced Course
1.6   Folklore didactic   ⎭

1.1   **CONCEPT OF FOLKLORE.** A science that studies a specific act that is primarily characterized as anonymous, noninstitutionalized, and eventually as being old, functional, and prelogical.

1.1.1. The folkloric meaning of the term "anonymous" is the same as defined in the dictionaries. *Anonymous, a, um,* that which has no name or which conceals it; adjective, without the author's name.

1.1.2. *Noninstitutionalized* is an expression taken from pedagogy to distinguish instruction that is neither organized, controlled, nor graduated. Folklore is transmitted along this route, one which is not official, universitarian, nor aristocratic.

1.1.3. *Old,* like anonymous, has the same meaning as its literal meaning.

1.1.4. *Functional* comes from *functio, onis, ar,* that is to say, it performs a function. The function is the objective that justifies the culture's existence, its reason for being. It will be understood, however, that "cultural changes" are due to their function. Culture undergoes change constantly so as to achieve better "functional," performance, to be more satisfying. "Motivations" and "function," however, are inalterable factors from generation to generation. Culture is what changes. It is supremely dynamic.

1.1.5. *Prelogical,* the term introduced by Lévy-Bruhl to the social sciences, that act whose relationship to causality is infantile; that is, it functions with primary forms and contrary to Aristotelian logic. Acts are prelogical because they are controlled by emotions and not by scientific reason.

1.2   **FIELD FOLKLORE**

1.2.1. **PHASES**

1.2.1.1. *Observation.* The exteriority, coerciveness, functionality, and interdependence of the socio-cultural act.

1.2.1.2. *Collection.* Abstraction, "integral collection," and "participant research."

1.2.1.3. *Criticism.* The removal of "preconceived notions" and "ideologies."
1.2.1.4. *Classification.* What it consists of and its use.
1.2.1.5. *Interpretation.* Need for knowledge of theories and their a posteriori application. The discovery of laws.
1.2.1.6. *Utilization.* Intervention in the social order.
1.2.2.   TECHNIQUES.
1.2.2.1. *Techniques of putting a plan into execution.* The selection of tasks, the development of questionnaires, the tour plan.
1.2.2.2. *Techniques for coming into contact with the act and the informant.* Practical advice.
1.2.2.3. *Techniques for card-indexing and classifying.* Value of field notebook.
1.2.2.4. *Techniques for criticizing the card index.* Composition of the report and how to insure the fidelity of the act.
1.2.2.5. *The Team's director.* Concept and tasks.
1.3   FACTUAL FOLKLORE. The portion of General Folklore that studies the different categories of folkloric acts that I classify in six groups and one *addendum:* The Folkloric Calendar.
1.3.1.   Folkloric Calendar.
1.3.2.   Poetic Folklore.
1.3.3.   Narrative Folklore.
1.3.4.   Linguistic Folklore.
1.3.5.   Magical Folklore.
1.3.6.   Social Folklore.
1.3.7.   Ergological Folklore.
1.3.1.   FOLKLORIC CALENDAR. The chronological, geographic, descriptive, brief, bibliographic, and documentary listing of folkloric feasts. It serves as a plan for the researcher, a master of techniques, who will not only succeed in obtaining data on the feast itself but also on themes that are not preferentially displayed such as certain legends and tales.
1.3.2.   POETIC FOLKLORE.
1.3.2.1. Song collections.
1.3.2.2. Ballad collections.
1.3.2.3. Proverb collections.
1.3.2.4. Riddle collections.

1.3.2.1.   COLLECTIONS OF SONGS.
1.3.2.1.1.   Collections of Children's Songs.
    A. Early infancy.
       1. Cradle.
       2. Affectionate playing.*
       3. Mnemonic
    B. Infancy in conflict.
       4. Allusion.
       5. Chance.
       6. Deception.
       7. *Ex-libris.*
       8. Repartees.
       9. Tongue twisters.
    C. Infancy in agreement.
      10. Eliminating formulas or counts.
      11. Embololalia and glossolalia.
      12. Occurrences.
      13. Rounds.
1.3.2.1.2.   Adult Songs.
      14. Drink and drugs.
      15. Loose quatrains.
      16. Nondramatic dances.
      17. Dramatics.
      18. Folk-latinisms.
      19. History and politics.
      20. Games.
      21. Praises.
      22. Magic and Religion.
      23. "Payadas."**
      24. "Pontos."†
      25. Vendors' cries.
      26. "Relaciones."††
      27. Improvisations.

---

*In Spanish: "mimo." "Brinco" in Portuguese.
**Payada*. Spanish expression meaning a debate sung generally between two folk singers.
  †*Ponto*. Sung evocation of Afro-Brazilian saints.
  ††*Relaciones*. Term of Rio de la Plata folklore. Type of verse sung alternately by a couple during pauses in a dance tune.

1.3.4.1.5.   Barbarisms. (Errors in morphology.)
1.3.4.1.6.   Redundancy. (Repetition of the same aspects, episodes or opinions.)
1.3.4.2.   Toponyms.
1.3.4.3.   Vocabulary in general.
1.3.4.4.   Nicknames.
1.3.4.5.   Slang.
1.3.4.6.   Vendor's cries.
1.3.4.7.   Imitations.
1.3.5.   MAGICAL FOLKLORE.
1.3.5.1.   *Magic properly stated.*
1.3.5.1.1.   Nonmedicinal.
    A.   Divinatory (good, bad, events).
    B.   Contagious (good, bad, prophylaxis).
    C.   Imitative (good, bad, prophylaxis).
1.3.5.1.2.   Medicinal.
    A.   Contagious (good, bad, prophylaxis)
    B.   Imitative (good, bad, prophylaxis)
    C.   Plant.
    D.   Scatological.
1.3.5.   *Animism.*
1.3.5.2.1.   Crosses.
1.3.5.2.2.   Wake.
1.3.5.2.3.   Mourning.
1.3.5.2.4.   Burial.
1.3.5.3.   *Religion.*
1.3.5.3.1.   Charism.
1.3.5.3.2.   Independent Catholicism.
1.3.5.3.3.   Official Catholicism (its folkloric aspects).
1.3.5.3.4.   Afro-American religions.
1.3.5.4.   *Totemism.*
1.3.5.4.1.   Zoomorphic.
1.3.5.4.2.   Phytomorphic.
1.3.5.5.   *Fetishism.*
1.3.5.5.1.   Ornithomorphic.
1.3.5.5.2.   Phytomorphic.
1.3.5.5.3.   Zoomorphic.
1.3.5.5.4.   Verbal.
1.3.5.5.5.   Poikilmorphic.

1.3.5.6. *Tabooism.*
1.3.5.6.1. Ornithomorphic.
1.3.5.6.2. Objects.
1.3.5.6.3. Acts, etc.
1.3.5.7. Beliefs. Folkloric pieces that are not exactly samples of the "omnipotence of ideas," whether animistic, religious, totemistic, or fetishistic. Pieces that are not to harm nor to do good nor to cure, and that are not preventive. Generally, there are neither mimicry, numerical, nor verbal values in them. They do not answer the questions who? what? or why? They are traditional suppositions stated spontaneously in narrative form on specific occasions. For this very reason, their research data almost always occurs by chance between pieces of other dispositions.
1.3.6. SOCIAL FOLKLORE.
1.3.6.1. *Feasts.*
1.3.6.1.1. From independent Catholicism.
1.3.6.1.2. From official Catholicism (patronal and nonpatronal).
1.3.6.1.3. From African religions.
1.3.6.1.4. Carnival.
1.3.6.1.5. Civic celebrations. (Folkloric aspects.)
1.3.6.2. *Dramatic acts.* Folkloric representations that are characterized by the following principal traits: (1) Struggle of good over evil. (2) Death and resurrection, and for the following secondary features: (3) cortege (4) stage (5) religious origin (6) comicality (7) influence of the struggle for life (8) presence of the semieducated elements (Mário de Andrade).
1.3.6.3. *Independent Music and Dance.*
1.3.6.4. *Games*
1.3.6.4.1. Competitive Games in which animals participate.
A. Horse races.
B. Bull fights.
1.3.6.4.2. Competition among people alone.
1.3.6.4.3. Games of chance.
1.3.6.4.4. Games for amusement.
1.3.6.4.5. *Clothing, disguises, and folk characters.*
1.3.6.5.1. Disguises.

1.4.1. FOLKLORE AND PSYCHOANALYSIS. The study of the relationship between these two disciplines in which the folkloric expressions of the following psychoanalytical aspects are minutely described:

1.4.1.9. Symbolism.
1.4.2. FOLKLORE AND EDUCATION. A study of the relationship between these two disciplines in which serviceable folkloric items are described in minute detail as well as rejected folkloric items, that is to say, those that should be pursued and destroyed.
1.4.2.1. *Serviceable folklore.*
1.4.2.1.1. Ethical acts.
1.4.2.1.2. Aesthetic acts.
1.4.2.1.3. Test acts.
1.4.2.1.4. Imaginative acts.
1.4.2.1.5. Mnemonic acts.
1.4.2.1.6. Motivating acts.
1.4.2.1.7. Acts of confraternization.
1.4.2.2. *Rejected folklore.*
1.4.2.2.1. Genital acts.
1.4.2.2.2. Scatological acts.
1.4.2.2.3. Para-scatological acts.
1.4.2.2.4. Para-psychopathological acts.
1.4.2.2.5. Aggressive acts.

12

Classifications of Factual Folklore

As a result of our array of the various aspects of folkloric science in a schematic diagram, we have now identified the proper place of the "Concept of Folklore." This has led to an understanding that folkloric acts are of several types. I must emphasize, for the information of the reader, that there is no unanimity of opinion on the order or methodological arrangement of these types. There is no single system of classification, and we will never have one for the simple reason that classifications are merely resources that we use in given situations. In themselves, they are a means to an end and not an end. They vary of necessity, and the variations are as numerous as the different situations demand. They are but a point of departure, a theoretical structure.

Many scholars share this point of view. Renato Almeida stated, "Classifications have a summary value for me. They are pragmatic and are useful for expediting interviews, for keeping files and documentation in general. Living elements, like folkloric acts, cannot be subjected to schematic categorization. They are mutually intertwined so that the study is always an approximation" (2). According to Julio Caro Baroja, "an excessive tendency to formal classification may lead to stagnation and weakness" (26, p. 230). Hoyos Sáinz feels the same way, "Overly complex classifications are not very useful because they fragment legitimate unities of thought and action" (60, p. 268). In addition to these authors, consult Van Gennep on this topic (121, pp. 72–74). Nevertheless, there could be a middle-of-the-road attitude in folklore that shares all classifications yet devised and still to come.

Personally, and as a result of my years of dedication to this science, I have come to separate folkloric acts into six groups: (1) Poetic Folklore; (2) Narrative Folklore; (3) Linguistic Folklore; (4) Magic Folklore; (5) Social Folklore; and (6) Ergological Folklore. Due to its brevity and coherence, this classification has provided extraordinary results in teaching and in research. For this reason, I recommend it to the reader even though doing so may reflect little modesty.

The following are other examples of classification from the many in existence: This system is from Saintyves:

I. Material Life. (Acts related to the very needs of existence, according to Alfredo Poviña: 1. Clothing 2. Food 3. Adornments 4. Work, etc.)

II. Spiritual Life. (Acts related to intellectual needs based on the beautiful, the sacred, as well as the different forms of popular wisdom, according to Poviña.)

III. Social Life.

1. Institutions. (Associations, family, et cetera.)

Boggs develops his system according to the manner in which the acts are transmitted:

I. By means of the spoken word.
    1. Literary Folklore.
        A. Legends.
        B. Myths.
        C. Traditions.
    2. Linguistic Folklore. (Acts from the speech of people, from plebeian language.)
        A. Proverbs.
        B. Sayings.
        C. Prophecies.
    3. Scientific Folklore.
        A. Beliefs.
        B. Superstitions.
        C. Riddles.
II. By means of imitative acts of man.
    1. Music and dance.
    2. Games, customs or uses, et cetera.

Poviña, our reference for the classifications of Saintyves and Boggs, in turn gives his own system established on basic human faculties: intelligence, emotions, and volition.

I. Acts associated with intelligence.
  1. Fables.
  2. Tales.
  3. Legends.
  4. Myths, et cetera.
II. Acts associated with emotions.
  1. Music, et cetera.
III. Acts associated with social activity. (Folklore of volition.)
  1. Practices.
  2. Customs, et cetera (93, pp. 650–668).

Jacovella prefers the following:

I. Intellectual or animological folklore.
  1. Arts.
    A. Literature in verse and prose.
    B. Music.
    C. Dance.
    D. Sculpture.
    E. Decoration.
  2. Concept of the world.
    A. Beliefs and rituals.
  3. Knowledge (of man and of nature).
II. Social or sociological folklore.
  1. Language.
  2. Practices and customs.
  3. Feasts and ceremonies.
III. Material or ergological folklore.
  1. Basic techniques.
    A. Productive (agriculture, animal husbandry, hunting, fishing).
    B. Preservation.
    C. Preparation.
    D. Disposition.
  2. Transforming techniques.
    A. Textiles
    B. Leather.
    C. Wood.
    D. Other animal and vegetable elements.
    E. Clay.

    F.   Metals.

    G. The dwelling place and its annexes; furnishing and domestic utensils.

    H. Wearing apparel.

    I.   Means of transportation: riding accoutrements.

    J.   Occupations and professions: animal tamer, urban folk medicine man, singer, tracker, artisans of various kinds— silversmith, blacksmith, weaver.

  3. Corporal techniques.

    A. Horseback riding.

    B. Swimming.

    C. Fencing.

We could reproduce the classifications of Thoms, Charlote Burne, Sébillot, E. Hoffman-Krayer, Melvil Dewey, Puymaigre, Gomme, and many other ancient and modern scholars. In addition to the previously cited sources, I recommend the following on this topic: 67, pp. 28–32, 83–101; 87; 18, pp. 8, 9; 21, pp. 56–58; 62, p. 26; 122, p. 89 and those following; 106, pp. 33–35; 81, pp. 21–23, 41–73, 76, 79, 82, 99 and those following; 83, pp. 41, 73, 76, 79, 82, 99 and those following; 82; 85, p. 328.

The same proliferation exists in subsectional aspects of folklore such as: songs, ballads, proverbs, riddles, myths, legends, tales, experiences, magic, and religion. Let us, at random, take one example: Renato Almeida's classification of Brazilian songs:

    I.   Sentimental songs:

       1. *Modinhas.*

   II. Lyrical-narrative songs:

       1. Ballads.

       2. *Xácaras.*

       3. Guitar *Modas.*

  III. Malicious songs:

       1. *Lundus.*

       2. *Emboladas.*

       3. *Chulas.*

  IV. Religious songs:

       1. Catholic:

     A. Liturgical:
        1) Litanies.
        2) Benedictions.
     B. Popular:
        1) Hymns of San Gonzalo.
        2) Pilgrim Songs.
        3) Prayers to make it rain.
  2. Fetishist:
     A. *Candomblé* songs.
     B. *Catimbó* chants.
V. Satirical:
  1. Challenges.
  2. Martelos.*
VI. Work songs:
  1. Publications by criers.
  2. Work songs.
  3. Cowboys chants.
VII. Recreation:
  1. Drinking songs (toasts, *coretos*, et cetera).
  2. Sports (like those of the *capoeira*).
VIII. Military:
  1. Songs of recruits.
  2. Barracks' songs.
IX. Infantine songs:
  1. Lullabies.
  2. Play songs. (1, p. 17)

I will conclude by stating that although the topic of the classification of factual folklore is basic and important, it is not transcendental. The reader can elect the one that seems best to him. The same is not true with the concept of Folklore since it strives to achieve complete unity.

---

*Martelos. Stanza of from six to ten decasyllabic lines very popular in poetic duels of the popular Brazilian folk poets. These duels are called *desafios* in Brazil, that is *payada, palla,* in some Spanish-American countries.

13

The Teaching of General Folklore

Now that we have seen the place of the "Concept of Folklore" in the study of General Folklore let us look at its hierarchical position in the Didactic of Folklore. At the present time, I divide the teaching of General Folklore into two large areas: basic and advanced. The basic course of General Folklore has three levels: the first contains the "Concept and Generalities of Folklore," the second "Field Folklore" or "Folkloric Research," and the third "Factual Folklore" or "Species of Folklore." The advanced course of General Folklore must embrace at least three other minimal levels: the first is "Interdisciplinary Folklore" or "Relationships of Folklore," the second is the "History of Folklore," and the third is "Folklore Didactic."

This sequence is a response to a logical order of questions. Any change of order here causes unusual problems not only for the student but for the teacher as well. Each one of these areas then has its own specific objectives. The basic course prepares the student for the advanced course and provides him with the data for him to successfully take advantage of it. The advanced course provides for the in-depth development of knowledge. It is not absolutely necessary for those who prefer to dedicate themselves to field research. It is essential, however, for those who hope to earn the title of "professor" of General Folklore.

Choosing the subject matter for each of these disciplines is a problem less open to discussion. Folklorists the world over are fairly well agreed as to what should be taught under the headings "Concept and Generalities," "Field Folklore," "Factual Folklore," and "Interdisciplinary Folklore." The theoretical position concerning the intrinsic meaning of these themes is all that varies. There are many ways of stating the concept of Folklore, various research techniques on acts, various individual ideas concerning species and the relationships of Folklore, and various points of view on this or that theory and many pedagogical-folkloric discussions.

We here state, albeit, in a rather synthetic form, the principal points dealt with in each discipline. The general characteristics of the folkloric act are treated within the "Concept" course. Then the boundaries of Folklore are dealt with, as Folklore relates to other sciences. In the "Generalities" course, we include the ideas relative to the creation of the word "folklore" including a consideration of the propriety of the term, other proposed terms, definitions, and the importance of the study of folklore. "Field Folklore," the teaching of its phases and techniques, is an important part of theory and practice. These phases correspond to the phases of science in general, with appropriate thematic variants: observation, compilation, criticism, classification, and interpretation. The techniques of field folklore involve establishing contact with the act and its informants, card-indexing, classification, and the criticism of card indexes. A few words concerning the team leader, his rights and obligations complete the topic (29).

"Factual Folklore" comes immediately afterward. We must make it clear, nevertheless, that we alternate research with the study of the species in accordance with pedagogical needs. If this were not done, the professor would not be able to keep the students in the lecture hall for long. "Factual Folklore" is unlimited and quite enjoyable. In this respect, it differs from the study of folklore's concept which requires greater acuteness on the part of the student. With the study of the species, he comes in contact with a variety of examples of universal folklore and concerns himself with knowing and identifying those in his own area, even many acts recalled from childhood.

These species may be cataloged in the following families of acts: oral literature, linguistic folklore, magic folklore, social folklore, and ergological folklore. Oral literature includes the poetic aspect (songs, ballads, proverbs, and riddles) and the narrative (myths, legends, tales, events, and jokes). Magic folklore includes: magic in its strictest sense, animism, religion, totemism, fetishism, and tabooism. Social folklore includes: music and dance, feasts, games, costumes, folk characters, family institutions, and so on. And ergological folklore includes: preservation techniques (food, dwelling, et cetera), transforming techniques (popular art, transportation, et cetera) and other techniques.

The advanced Folklore course begins at the outset with the very complex field of interpretation as it applies to psychoanalysis, education, criminology, Marxism, and other theories and doctrines. Each interrelated study requires months of explanation and discussion in seminars to attain the desired objectives. The knowledge of psychoanalytical folklore, for example, must at least include a study of the theory of psychoanalysis and folkloric casuistry. I wrote *Folklore and Psychoanalysis* as the result of such a course that I gave at the University of Uruguay in 1954. I explained psychoanalytical theory using folkloric examples and studied the theory of the libido, the structure and mechanism of the psychic system, and the collective subconscious. Then we developed casuistic correspondents: folkloric casuistry of oral libido, anal libido, genital libido, narcissism, the Oedipus complex and identification, infantile fantasies on birth, the castration and anguish complex, symbolism, and the mechanisms of the psychic system.

The advanced Folklore course is completed by the "History of Folklore" and the "Teaching of Folklore." In "History of Folklore," we analyze ancient theories, philological and allegorical, the naturists, the historicalists and diffusionists, the anthropological and psychological, the ritualists and liturgicalists, and recent schools up until the present time taking as a principal model Arthur Ramos' excellent text *Estudos de Folk-lore,* published in 1952.

Concerning the "Teaching of Folklore," we find ourselves still completely in the period of prior studies. There really does not exist a manual on Folklore didactics in the Americas, so there is everything to be accomplished in this field. (Ismael Moya's book *Didáctica del Folklore* has a title that does not relate to its contents.) Until the present time, we have assigned everything referring to the value of methodology, critical bibliographies, anthologies, and museums to Folklore didactics, the final course in the career of the folklorologist.

The teaching of General Folklore is already reality in many American countries. Its development will dissipate the mistaken ideas surrounding folklore of a large part of the general public and will lead to a scientific understanding of social acts by all people in every region.

14

"Folklore"

As a complement to the study of the concept of Folklore, let us look at some aspects of the origin of the term "Folklore." It must be obvious that I am directing the contents of this section to individuals who have never previously come in contact with our science. My sole purpose is to throw light on the subject since we are dealing with a commonplace matter covered in every beginner's manual.

THE FOLKLORIC ACT IS ANTERIOR TO FOLKLORE

Authors of treatises carefully point out that Folklore was being studied long before the creation of the term "Folklore" in 1846. Concerning this, Hoyos Sáinz says, "more than in any other discipline, although lacking in methodization, there was, in Folklore, data concerning the act itself . . ." (60, p. 5). This author immediately recommends Guichot y Sierra's book for those wishing to have an idea of the development of folkloric studies during this first period. In this work, *Noticia Histórica del Folklore, Orígenes en todos los países hasta 1890* published in Seville in 1922, Guichot y Sierra develops the following outline:

First era: Eighteenth century until Neo-classicism.

Second era: End of the eighteenth century until mid-nineteenth century (the period of romanticism).

Third era: (period of realism) is divided into two sub-periods:

1. The period of regionalist preparation, until 1875.

2. The Folklorist period, until 1890.

Present era: The Scientific era of Folklore (60, pp. 5–6).

Moya does not agree with Hoyos Sáinz and prefers not to state that the methodization of Folklore began in 1846. According to Moya, the only contribution Thoms made was to develop the term. Moya says that Thomas should not at any time be credited with having pioneered the systematization of our discipline, since "a science is not created in a day, nor is it born from a word like Minerva from Jupiter's brain." Moya believed that the structuring of folkloric science has been going on "since men took note of the traditional clutter of the people." He continues, "The subject of folklore was studied for centuries without calling it folklore. And it became a science" (84, pp. 14–15). To illustrate his judgment, he cited some authors from the past who wrote chapters or books on Folklore: Erasmus (*Adagia*), Pausanias, Aristoteles, Donatus, Soraphan de Rieros (*Medicina española contenida en proverbios vulgares de nuestra lengua,* 1616), Hesiod (*Works and Days*), Euhemerus (*Sacred History*), Fabricius, Juan de Mal Lara (*Philosophia Vulgar,* 1524–1571), Gonzalo Correas, Pedro Mexía (*La Silva de Varia Elección,* 1542), Rodrigo Caro (seventeenth century), Giovanni Battista Vico (1686–1774, *Scienza Nuova*), Johann Gottfried von Herder (1744–1803, *Volkslieder*). Moya's conclusion is categorical, "Let us opportunely leave the glory to William John Thoms, the worthy archeologist, of having found a word in the Anglo-Saxon vocabulary that will be the name of the science which, according to Gomme, deals with survivances in contemporary environments. But let us not credit him with having fathered this discipline because it is as ancient as the common people" (84, p. 20).

I feel that both Hoyos Sáinz and Moya are correct and that they only lacked completing their rationales. Hoyos could have agreed that there were certain scientific ideas among those scholars of the past instead of merely considering them as disorganized antecedents of present-day progress. Moya, in turn, would have been more prudent if he had explained that many of the works of the previously cited precursors were no more than aesthetic projections and not scientific works.

WILLIAM JOHN THOMS (1803–1885)

William John Thoms was born in Westminster, England, according to the data contained in the works of Ralph Steele Boggs.

His father was a Treasury Department employee and he was a clerk in the Chelsea Hospital secretary's office. He was interested in bibliography and the study of antiquities from the time of his youth. He married Laura Sale, a musician's daughter, and they had three sons and six daughters. In 1838 he became a member of the Antiquarian Society, and, as secretary of the Camden Society from 1838 to 1873, he published works on this subject. He founded a journal *Notes and Inquiries* in 1849, and was its first publisher until 1872. In 1834 he published his *Songs and Legends of France, Spain, Tartary and Ireland,* and *Songs and Legends of Germany.* He died August 15, 1885.

His fame in the history of Folklore is no doubt due to his probable creation of the term "Folk-lore." Elieser Edward set out to research the truth of the matter. Finally, in his *Words, Facts, and Phrases* in 1881, he stated that really the first time the word "Folklore" appeared in print was in the English newspaper *Athenaeum.*

In *Athenaeum* No. 982, Saturday, August 22, 1846, there appeared a letter from William John Thoms, under the pseudonym Ambrose Merton, titled "Folklore." The letter became famous and many specialized journals have reproduced it. Here it is:

> Your pages have so often given evidence of the interest which you take in what we in England designate as Popular Antiquities, or Popular Literature (though by-the-bye it is more a Lore than a Literature, and would be most aptly described by a good Saxon compound, Folklore—the Lore of the People)—that I am not without hopes of enlisting your aid in garnering the few ears which are remaining, scattered over that field from which our forefathers might have gathered a goodly crop.
>
> No one who has made the manners, customs, observances, superstitions, ballads, proverbs, etc., of the olden time his study, but must have arrived at two conclusions:—the first, how much that is curious and interesting in these matters is now entirely lost —the second, how much may yet be rescued by timely exertion. What Hone endeavoured to do in his "Everyday Book," etc., *The Athenaeum,* by its wider circulation, may accomplish ten times more effectually—gather together the infinite number of minute facts, illustrative of the subject I have mentioned, which are scattered over the memories of its thousands of readers, and preserve them in its pages, until some James Grimm shall arise who shall do for the Mythology of the British Islands the good service which that profound antiquary and philologist has accomplished for the Mythology of Germany. The present century has scarcely produced a

more remarkable book, imperfect as its learned author confesses
it to be, than the second edition of the *Deutsche Mythologie:* and,
what is it?—a mass of minute facts, many of which, when separately
considered, appear trifling and insignificant,—but, when taken
in connection with the system into which his master-mind has
woven them, assume a value that he who first recorded them never
dreamed of attributing to them.

How many such facts would one word from you evoke, from the
north and from the south—from John O'Groat's to the Land's
End! How many readers would be glad to show their gratitude for
the novelties which you, from week to week, communicate to them,
by forwarding to you some record of old Time—some recollection
of a now neglected custom—some fading legend, local tradition,
or fragmentary ballad!

Nor would such communications be of service to the English
antiquary alone. The connection between the *folklore* of England
(remember I claim the honor of introducing the epithet Folklore,
as Disraeli does of introducing Fatherland, into the literature of
this country) and that of Germany is so intimate that such communications will probably serve to enrich some future edition of
Grimm's mythology.

Let me give you an instance of this connection—In one of the
chapters of Grimm, he treats very fully of the parts which the
Cuckoo plays in Popular Mythology—of the prophetic character
with which it has been invested by the voice of the people; and
gives many instances of the practice of deriving predictions from
the number of times which its songs is heard. He also records a
popular notion, "that the Cuckoo never sings till he has thrice
eaten his fill of cherries." Now, I have lately been informed of a
custom which formerly obtained among children in Yorkshire,
that illustrates the fact of a connection between the Cuckoo and
the Cherry,—and that, too, in their prophetic attributes. A friend
has communicated to me that children in Yorkshire were formerly
(and may be still) accustomed to sing round a cherry-tree the
following invocation:—

> Cuckoo, Cherry-tree,
> Come down and tell me
> How many years I have to live.

Each child then shook the tree,—and the number of cherries which
fell betokened the years of its future life.

The Nursery Rhyme which I have quoted, is, I am aware, well
known. But the manner in which it was applied is not recorded by
Hone, Brand, or Ellis: and is one of those facts, which, trifling in
themselves, become of importance when they form links in a great
chain—one of those facts which a word from *The Athenaeum* would

gather in abundance for the use of future inquiries into that interesting branch of literary antiquities,—our Folklore.

Ambrose Merton

P.S.—It is only honest that I should tell you I have long been contemplating a work upon our *Folklore* (under *that title,* mind Messrs. A, B, and C,—so do not try to forestall me) ;—and I am personally interested in the success of the experiment which I have, in this letter, albeit imperfectly, urged you to undertake (116, pp. 4–6).

Van Gennep notes that, by this letter, Thoms tried to eliminate the use of Brand's expression, "Popular Antiquities," which appeared in 1795 (121, I, p. 6). And he succeeded in doing so.

THE ETYMOLOGY OF FOLK-LORE

In his *Estudos de Folclore,* Antonio Osmar Gomes cites the historical-etymological analysis of the expression "Folk-lore" by Gustavo Barroso. Folklore has its origin in *Bal,* a celtic root which means "strength, multitude." This root changed prosodically to *val,* was introduced into the Oscan language and later Latin. Here it was trifurcated, giving the word *Valere* (to feel well, to enjoy good health, to be strong, to be worth something before one's peers), the word *Vallare* (to enclose with walls, barricades, to fortify); and, finally, the word *vulgare* (to diffuse, to publish, to divulge) and its derivatives. Among these derivatives, we find the word *Vulgo.* And from *Vulgo,* later came the word *Volk* in German and *folk* in English (91).

This etymological evolution interests us as a means of establishing the common geneology of the terms *Vulgo, Volk,* and *Folk.* We can even make the following scheme:

1. Vulgos (Latin)=Vulgo (Spanish)=Folk (English)=Das Volk (German);
2. Demos, Ethnos, Laos, Anthropos (Greek)=Populus, Plebs (Latin)=Peuple (French)=Pueblo, Colectividad (Spanish)=People (English);
3. Logos (Greek)=Connaitre, Connaissance (French)=Conocimiento (Spanish)=Learning (English)=Lehre (German);
4. Lore (English)=Kunde (German).

By consulting this chart, we can better understand the polemics surrounding the word folklore. These are the same ones surrounding the roots *Volk* and *Lore*.

Das Volk is, in fact, collectivity, people but not all the people, rather those that are unlearned or the *Vulgus* as conceptualized by Cervantes: "And do not think my lord, that I only call the plebeian and humble people vulgar, since all that are unlearned, even though they be lords and princes must be numbered among the vulgar." The Volks-Vulgus ideological relationship satisfies many scholars, and Imbelloni even wrote a chapter entitled "The *Folk* is the *Vulgus*" (62, p. 42).

On the other hand, *Kunde* in German comes close to the meaning of *Lore* in English. *Das Volk* cannot be translated as *People* nor can *Kunde* be translated as *Learning*. "People's Learning" means institutionalized learning by the people, the collectivity. *Volks-kunde* or *Folk-lore* is in turn translated by knowledge, the knowledge, of course, of the *Vulgo*, the lore of the Vulgo, that is a certain kind of knowledge. We only need the following appraisal from Boggs concerning this to understand what is meant and to completely master the English meaning: "It is worth pointing out that this second English expression "Lore" has a special shade of meaning because it identifies nonscientific, private, traditional knowledge and is equivalent for us to plebeian (vulgar) knowledge. It is different from learning which also signifies knowledge, but which refers to knowledge in relation to the level of culture, to erudition, in conclusion the knowledge of the culture" (93, p. 150).

PROPOSED LABELS

There was no lack of those who denied any value in *Kunde* and *Volk,* and perhaps mixed them up with *Lehre*. From such a denial, it was easy to begin the development of other terms to substitute for *Volkskunde* or *Folklore*. They had recourse to Greek and invented *Demótica* (Théophilo Braga), *Demopedia* (Mariano de Cavia), *Demopsychology* and *Demology* (the Italians) (84, pp. 22–23; 70, p. 69). The Spaniard, Julio Cejador y Frauca or the Mexican Basauri created *Demosophy* (70, p. 69; 56, p. 98) which is no doubt inappropriate because *sophy* equates with knowledge at its highest level of meaning, that is, in its philosophical meaning. The *Vulgus* cannot cope with *sophy*, since it lacks fundamentals for this. *Laos* exists in Greece where a group founded *Laography*, a journal "dedicated to the study of modern Greek and comparative folklore" (121, p. 9).

Some scholars prefer to take "Tradition" as a point of departure instead of *Vulgus*. And so "Traditionism" (Beaurepaire-Froment) and *Trademology* (Moya) were developed (106, p. 22; 84, p. 23). Although we are living in a period of field research, this matter interests many scholars. For example, in Brazil nationalist authors continue to struggle to apply the term Populário (115, p. 17).

PROPRIETY AND IMPEDIMENTS OF THE TERM "FOLKLORE"

In spite of the reactions against it, the facts are that this word was adopted. The Mexican José de J. Núñez y Domínguez attending the First International Folklore Congress held in Paris in 1937, stated that it was adopted there by unanimous vote (87, p. 257). This does not mean, however, that all controversy concerning it had been resolved. The term was most probably accepted due to the failings of the others. "Folklore" has flexibility: it can be used for the formation of folklorist, folklorologist, folklorically, folklorism, to folklorize, folklorizing, and so on (81, p. 18). Javier Guerrero uses "folklorology" (56, p. 99). And, as Ramos has pointed out, it is used in combinations such as Christ-lore, plant-lore, Folksong, Folk-dance, and Folk-speech (98, p. 13). The other terms do not have this flexibility. Furthermore, even though there is a perfect correspondence between *Vulgus* and *Folk*, the use of *vulgolology* as well as *plebology, plegography,* and *populology* would sound awkward (121, p. 8). Van Gennep, who made this observation, states that he still sees no reason for rejecting the use of "folklore" for nationalistic reasons since so many other English words have been assimilated in the neo-Latin languages, such as *sport, turf, jockey, football.*

Another argument against the adoption of "folklore" says that the word does not differentiate between the science or the act, since both have the same name. That is, at times it means "lore of the folk" and on other occasions "lore about the folk" (62, p. 15). This problem can be solved as we have done throughout the book, by using a lowercase letter when we talk about the lore of the folk (folklore) and a capital letter when we talk about the science that deals with that lore (Folklore).

Appendix

LATIN AMERICAN STUDIES
ON GENERAL FOLKLORE

A brief list of books, pamphlets, and articles that have appeared in Latin America on general folklore may be helpful for the purpose of theoretical research, pedagogical application, or even just dissemination. These make up the foundation on which we Latin Americans erect the theoretical structure of our discipline.

There are many titles omitted from this list. My objective, however, is to show the reader that Latin America is not as poor as it used to be in folkloric studies. On the other hand, it suggests that an essay based on the critical analysis of these texts will reveal the existence of an authentic Latin American folklore thought even though it may still be in the midst of its formative stage. Often one hears that America has not produced any philosophers and that, consequently, it does not have any philosophical thought of its own. In a few years, it will not be possible to say this about American folkloric thought since America has already produced many advances over Europe.

1939

Jijena Sánchez, Rafael y Jacovella, Bruno. *Las supersticiones. Contribución a la metodología de investigación folklórica.* Buenos Aires; Ediciones B. Aires, 1939. 154 pp.

1942

Jijena Sánchez, Rafael. *Instrucciones generales para la recolección del material folklórico.* Tucumán: Argentina, Universidad Nacional de Tucumán, Instituto de Historia, lingüística y folklore, 1942. 8 pp.

1943

Boggs, Ralph Steele, "El folklore, definición." México: *Anuario de la Sociedad Folklórica de México,* III, 1942, México, 1943, pp. 7–16.
Cadilla de Martínez, María. "El folklore." México, *Anales de la Sociedad Folklórica de México,* III, 1942, México: 1943, pp. 43–66.

Imbelloni, J. *Concepto y praxis del folklore como ciencia.* Buenos Aires: Editorial Humanior, 1943, 136 pp. w/illustrations. Reproduced in *Folklore Argentino,* Buenos Aires: Editorial Nova, 1959. 397 pp.

Poviña, Alfredo. *Sociología del Folklore.* Córdoba: Instituto de Arqueología, Lingüistica y Folklore "Dr. Pablo Cabrera," Universidad Nacional de Córdoba, No. XI. Reproduced in *Curso de sociología,* 2d Edition, Vol. II. Córdoba, Argentina: Editorial Assandri, 1950. 647 pp.

1944

Ribeiro, Joaquín. *Folklore brasileiro.* Rio de Janeiro: Livraria Editôra Zélio Valverde, 1944. 222 pp.

Vega, Carlos. *Panorama de la música popular argentina, con un ensayo sobre la ciencia del folklore.* Buenos Aires: Editorial Losada S. A., 1944. 361 pp.

1947

Molina Téllez, Félix. *El mito, la leyenda y el hombre.* Buenos Aires: Editorial Claridad, 1947. 298 pp. with illustrations.

Pereda Valdés, Ildefonso. *Cancionero popular uruguayo.* With a brief *Introduccion al estudio de la ciencia folklórica.* Montevideo: Editorial Florensa and Lafón, 1947, 201 pp.

1948

Almeida, Renato. "Métodos e classificações em folklore." Rio de Janeiro: *Jornal do Comércio.* August 22, 1948.

Boggs, Ralph Steele. "Lo Primitivo y lo material en el folklore." Buenos Aires: *Revista del Instituto Nacional de la Tradición.* Year I, no. 1, January–June 1948, pp. 30–38.

Boggs, Ralph Steele. "Classificação do conto popular." Rio de Janeiro: *Revista Cultura,* Year I, no. 1, September–December 1948, pp. 274–280.

Moya, Ismael. *Didáctica del folklore.* Buenos Aires: El Ateneo, 1948. 194 pp.

Osmar Gomes, Antônio. *"Estudos de folklore."* Rio de Janeiro: *Jornal do Comércio,* August 29, 1948.

1949

Cortazar, Augusto Raúl. *El carnaval en el folklore Calchaquí.* With a brief exposition on the Theory and Practice of the Integral Folkloric Method. Buenos Aires: Editorial Sudamericana, 1949, 289 pp.

1950

Carneiro, Édison. *Dinamica do folclore.* Rio de Janeiro: 1950, 80 pp.

Jijena Sánchez, Rafael. *El folklore. Sus métodos y sus conquistas.* Buenos Aires: *Primer Ciclo Anual de Conferencias,* Subsecretaria de Cultura de la Nación, 1950, pp. 217–241.

Morote Best, Efraín. *Elementos de folklore. Definición, contenido, procedimiento.* Cuzco: Universidad Nacional de Cuzco, Perú, 1950. 511 pp.

1951

Guerrero, Javier. "Consideraciones sobre folklore y ciencia folklórica." *Archivos Venezolanos de Folklore,* Year I, No. 1, pp. 43–103, January–June, 1951.

Jacovella, Bruno. *Manual-Guía para el recolector.* La Plata, Argentina: Instituto de la Tradición, 1951. 48 pp.

Lira, Mariza. *Migalhas folklóricas.* Rio de Janeiro: Edição da Gráfica Laemmert, Ltda., 1951. 200 pp.

Mata Machado Filho, Aires da. *Curso de folclore.* Rio de Janeiro: Livros de Portugal, 1951. 167 pp.

M. Román, Marcelino. *Sentido y alcance de los estudios folklóricos.* Paraná, Argentina: 1951. 62 pp.

1952

Câmara Cascudo, Luís da. *Literatura oral.* In the series *História da literatura brasileira,* edited by Álvaro Lins. Vol. VI, Rio de Janeiro: Livraria José Olympio Editôra, 1952. 465 pp.

Ramos, Arthur. *Estudos de Folk-Lore.* Preface by Roger Bastide. Rio de Janeiro: Livraria-Editôra da Casa do Estudante do Brasil, 1952. 191 pp.

Tavares de Lima, Rossini. *ABC de Folklore.* São Paulo: Publicação do Conservatório Dramático e Musical de São Paulo, 1952. 134 pp.

1954

Cabral, Oswaldo R. *Cultura e folclore. Bases científicas do folclore.* Preface by Roger Bastide. Santa Catarina: Edição da Comissão Catarinense de Folclore, 1954. 302 pp.

Cortazar, Augusto Raúl. "El folklore y su caraterización." Lima: *Folklore Americano,* Organ of the Comité Interamericano de Folklore, Year II, No. 2, 1954, pp. 42–43.

Cortazar, Augusto Raúl. *Qué es el folklore. Planteo y respuesta con especial referencia a lo argentino y americano.* Buenos Aires: Lajouane, 1954. 116 pp.

Morote Best, Efraín. *El Dr. Ralph Steele Boggs y su clasificación del folklore.* Cuzco: Universidad Nacional de Cuzco, 1954. 58 pp.

Poviña, Alfredo. *Teoría del folklore.* Córdoba: Editorial Assandri, 1954. 217 pp.

1956

Carvalho-Neto, Paulo de. *Concepto de folklore.* Montevideo: Editorial "Livraria Monteiro Lobato," 1956. 191 pp. Second Spanish edition, México: Editorial Pormaca, 1965. 180 pp.

Carvalho-Neto, Paulo de. *Folklore y psicoanálisis.* Preface by Roger Bas-

tide. Buenos Aires: Editorial Psique, 1956. 299 pp. Second Spanish
edition, México: Editorial mortíz, 1968. 250 pp.

1957

Almeida, Renato. *Inteligência do Folclore*. Rio de Janeiro: Livros de
Portugal, 1957. 310 pp.
Aretz, Isabel. *Manual de folklore venezolano*. Caracas: Ediciones del
Ministerio de Educación, 1957. 219 pp.

1958

Carvalho-Neto, Paulo de. *La investigación folklórica. Fases y Técnicas*.
Montevideo: Ministerio de Ganadería y Agricultura, Departamento
de Sociología Rural, 1958. 46 pp. mimeo. Reprinted in *Revista de
Filosofía, Letras y Educación*, No. 29, Quito: Editorial Universitaria,
1962. 45 pp.
Jacovella, Bruno C. "Los conceptos fundamentales clásicos del folklore.
Análisis y crítica." Montevideo, *Revista Sodre*, No. 6, December
1958, pp. 81–105. Reprinted in Buenos Aires, *Cuadernos del In-
stituto Nacional de Investigaciones Folklóricas*, no. 1, Ministerio de
Educación y Justicia, Dirección General de Cultura, 1960, pp. 27–48.

1959

Cortazar, Augusto Raúl. *Esquema del folklore*. Buenos Aires: Editorial
Columba, 1959. 63 pp.
Fernandes, Florestán. "Folclore e Ciências Sociais." São Paulo: *Revista
Brasiliense*, n. 24, 1959, pp. 133–151.

1960

Vega, Carlos. *La ciencia del folklore*. Buenos Aires: Editorial Nova, 1960.
254 pp.

1961

Seraine, Florival. *Para a metodologia da investigação folclórica*. Fortaleza:
Reprint from Boletim do Instituto de Antropologia da Universidade
do Ceará, 3, pp. 77–104. (1959) 1961.
Carvalho-Neto, Paulo de. *Folklore y Educación*. Preface by Gonzalo
Rubio Orbe. Quito: Editorial Casa de la Cultura Ecuatoriana, 1961.
315 pp. 2nd Spanish edition, Buenos Aires: Editorial Omeba, 1969.
272 pp.

1964

Barros, Raquel y Dannemann, M. *Guía metodológica de la investigación
folklórica*. Santiago: Reprint from *Revista Mapocho*, Tomo II, n. 1,
1964, pp. 168–178.
Cortazar, Augusto. *Concepción dinámica y funcional del folklore*. Madrid:
Reprint from "Homenaje a Fernando Márquez-Miranda," 1964, pp.
145–152 with 1 map.

Nascimento, Bráulio do. "Processos de variação do romance." Rio de Janeiro: *Revista Brasileira de Folclore,* Year IV, n. 8–10, 1964, pp. 59–126.

1965

Almeida, Renato. *Manual de coleta folclórica.* Rio de Janeiro: Campanha de Defesa do Folclore Brasileiro, 1965. 221 pp.

Câmara Cascudo, Luís da. "Introdução aos 'Folktales of Brazil'." Rio de Janeiro: *Revista Brasileira de Folclore,* Year V, n. 12, 1965, pp. 227–238.

1966

Nascimento, Bráulio de. "As sequências temáticas no romance tradicional." Rio de Janeiro: *Revista Brasileira de Folclore,* Year VI, n. 15, 1966, pp. 159–190.

1967

Chertudi, Susana. *El cuento folklórico.* Buenos Aires: Centro Editor de América Latina S.A., 1967. 58 pp.

1968

Rabaçal, Alfredo João. *Os conceitos de Folclore e Etnografia em Portugal e no Brasil.* Barcelos: Cadernos de Etnografia n. 5, 1968. 21 pp.

Bibliography

1. Almeida, Renato. *Esbóço de uma classificação de canções brasileiras.* Rio de Janeiro: CNFL, Doc. 11, April 13, 1948. 1 p. mimeographed.
2. Almeida, Renato. "Métodos e classificações em folklore." Rio de Janeiro: *Jornal do Comércio,* August 22, 1948.
3. Almeida, Renato. *Inteligência do folclore.* Rio de Janeiro: Livros de Portugal, 1957. 310 pp.
4. Alpert, Harry. *Emile Durkheim and his Sociology.* New York: Columbia University Press, 1939.
5. Alvarenga, Oneyda. *Música popular brasileña.* Translated by José Lión Depetre. México, Fondo de Cultura Económica, 1947. 272 pp.
6. Amaral, Amadeu. *Tradições populares.* With a study by Paulo Duarte. São Paulo: Instituto Progreso Editorial S. A., 1948. 418 pp.
7. Andrade, Mário de. "Folclore." In *Manual bibliográfico de estudos brasileiros,* edited by Rubens Borba de Moraes and William Berrien. Rio de Janeiro: Gráfica Editora Souza, 1949, pp. 285–317.
8. Angrand y Garaudy. *Curso elemental de filosofía.* Buenos Aires: Editorial Lautaro, 1947. 220 pp.
9. Arquivo Folclórico da Discoteca Pública Municipal. Vol. II. *Catálogo ilustrado do Museu Folklórico.* Organização de Oneyda Alvarenga. Sao Paulo: Prefeitura do Município de São Paulo, 1950. 295 pp.
10. Arquivo Folklórico da Discoteca Pública Municipal. Vol. I. *Melodias registradas por meios não-mecânicos.* Organização de Oneyda Alvarenga. São Paulo, 1946. 480 pp.
11. Azevedo, Fernando de. *Princípios de sociologia. Pequena introdução ao estudo de sociologia geral.* 3rd edition. São Paulo: Companhia Editôra Nacional, 1939. 433 pp.

12. Barbosa Lessa, L. C. *O sentido e o valor do tradicionalismo.* Porto Alegre: Comissão Estadual de Folclore do Rio Grande do Sul, 1954. 8 pp.
13. Barnes, Harry E., and Becker, Howard. *Social Thought From Lore to Science.* New York: Heath and Co., 1938. 2 vols. Vol. I, 790 pp; Vol. II, 1, 178 pp.
14. Barroso, Gustavo. *Mythes, contes et legéndes des indiens. Folk-lore Brésilien.* Paris: Libraire des Amateurs A. Ferroud, 1930. 79 pp.
15. Benedict, Ruth. *Race: Science and Politics.* New York: The Viking Press, 1945.
16. Boas, Franz. *Anthropology and Modern Life.* New York: W. W. Norton and Company, 1962.
17. Boggs, Ralph Steele. "Classificação do conto popular." Rio de Janeiro: *Revista Cultura,* Year I, no. 1, September–December 1948, pp. 274–280.
18. Boggs, Ralph Steele. "El folklore, definición." México, *Anuario de la Sociedad Folklórica de México,* Vol. III, 1942. México, 1943, pp. 7–16.
19. Boggs, Ralph Steele. *Enfermedades infantiles de la ciencia del folklore.* Coral Gables: University of Miami Press, *Folklore Americas,* Vol. XV, no. 1., June 1955. 6 pp.
20. Boggs, Ralph Steele. "Lo primitivo y lo material en el folklore." Buenos Aires: *Revista del Instituto Nacional de la Tradición,* Year I, no. 1, January–June 1948, pp. 30–38.
21. Cadilla de Martínez, María. "El Folklore," México: *Anales de la Sociedad Folklórica de México,* Vol. III, 1942, pp. 43–66 (1943).
22. Caillava, Domingo A. *Historia de la literatura gauchesca en el Uruguay.* Montevideo: Claudio García and Cía., 1945.
23. Câmara Cascudo, Luís da. *Literatura oral.* Rio de Janeiro: Livraria José Olympio Editôra, 1952. 465 pp.
24. Canto e Castro Mascarenhas Valdez, Manuel do. *Diccionario español-portugués.* Lisbon: Imprenta Nacional, Vols. I-II, 1864; Vol. II, 1866.
25. Carneiro, Édison. *Dinâmica do folclore.* Rio de Janeiro: 1950. 80 pp. 2nd edition, Rio de Janeiro: Editôra Civilização Brasileira S. A. 1965. 187 pp.
26. Caro Baroja, Julio. *Análisis de la cultura. Etnología, historia y folklore.* Barcelona: Centro de Estudios de Etnología Peninsular, 1949. 254 pp.
27. Carvalho-Neto, Paulo de. *Ensayo sobre los estudios folklóricos en el Paraguay.* Asunción: CEA, III Serie, Doc. 19, 1951. 43 pp. Mimeographed.
28. Carvalho-Neto, Paulo de. *Folklore y Psicoanálisis.* Buenos Aires: Editorial Psique, 1956. 299 pp. 2nd Spanish edition, México: Editorial Joaquín Mortíz, 1968.
29. Carvalho-Neto, Paulo de. *La investigación folklórica. Fases y*

técnicas. Montevideo: Ministerio de Ganadería y Agricultura. Departamento de Sociología Rural, no. 3, 1958. 46 pp. Mimeographed.

30. Cendrars, Blaise. *Antología negra.* Preface by Ortiz Oderigo. Buenos Aires: Ediciones Siglo Veinte, 1944. 353 pp.

31. Coluccio, Félix. *Folkloristas e instituciones folklóricas del mundo.* Prologues by Raffaele Corso and Alceu Maynard Araujo. Buenos Aires: Librería "El Ateneo," 1951. 157 pp.

32. Comas, Juan. *Racial Myths.* Paris: UNESCO, 1958. 51 pp.

33. Corso, Raffaele. "La nueva concepción del folklore." Tucumán: *Boletín de la Asociación Tucumana de Folklore,* 1951, Year I, January–February no. 9–10. 885 pp.

34. Cortazar, Augusto Raúl. *El carnaval en el folklore Chalchaquí. Con una breve exposición sobre la teoría y la práctica del método folklórico integral.* Buenos Aires: Editorial Sudamericana, 1949. 289 pp.

35. Cortazar, Augusto Raúl. "El folklore y su caracterización." Lima: *Folklore Americano,* Comité Interamericano de Folklore, Year II, no. 2, 1954, pp. 42–43.

36. Costa Eduardo, Octávio da. "O ensino dos conceitos básicos da Etnologia." São Paulo: *Revista Sociologia,* Vol. XI, no. 3, 1949, pp. 327–336.

37. Costa Pinto, Luiz de Aguiar. *Problemas sociais contemporaneos.* Mimeographed course. Rio de Janeiro: Faculdade Nacional de Filosofia, 1947.

38. Costa Pinto, Luiz de Aguiar. "Sociologia e mudança social." São Paulo, *Sociologia,* Vol. IX, no. 4, 1947, pp. 287–331.

39. Dias, Jorge. *Características do fato folclórico.* São Paulo: Congresso Internacional de Folclore, 1954. 7 pp. Mimeographed.

40. Discoteca Pública Municipal. *Babassuê. Registros sonoros de folclore musical brasileiro.* Vol. IV. Organização de Oneyda Alvarenga. São Paulo: Prefeitura do Município de São Paulo, 1950. 136 pp.

41. Discoteca Pública Municipal. *Catimbó. Registros sonoros de folclore musical brasileiro.* Vol. III. Organização de Oneyda Alvarenga. São Paulo: Prefeitura do Município de São Paulo, 1949. 217 pp.

42. Discoteca Pública Municipal. *Tambor-de-Mina e Tambor-de-Crioulo. Registros sonoros de folclore musical brasileiro.* Vol. II. Organização de Oneyda Alvarenga. São Paulo: Prefeitura do Município de São Paulo, 1948. 92 pp.

43. Discoteca Pública Municipal. *Xangô. Registros sonoros de folclore musical brasileiro.* Vol. I. Organização de Oneyda Alvarenga. São Paulo: Prefeitura do Município de São Paulo, 1948. 149 pp.

44. Durkheim, Émile. *The Division of Labor in Society.* Translated by George Simpson. Glencoe, Illinois: the Free Press, 1949.

45. Durkheim, Émile. *The Rules of Sociological Method,* 8th edition.

Translated by Sarah A. Solovay and John H. Mueller. Chicago: The University of Chicago Press, 1938. 146 pp.

46. Fernandes Braga, Henriqueta Rosa. O cancioneiro folclórico infantil e sua contribuição à música erudita. Rio de Janeiro: Semana Folclórica, 1948, pp. 47–63.

47. Fernandes, Florestán. "Lévy-Bruhl e o espírito científico." São Paulo: Revista de Antropologia, Vol. II, no. 2, December 1954, pp. 121–142.

48. Freud, Sigmund. An Outline of Psychoanalysis. Authorized translation by James Strachey, New York: W. W. Norton, 1949. 127 pp.

49. Freud, Sigmund. "On Narcissism: An Introduction." In Collected Papers. Authorized translation by Joan Riviere. London: The Hogarth Press, 1948. 508 pp.

50. Freud, Sigmund. A General Introduction to Psychoanalysis. Authorized English translation of the revised edition by Joan Riviere. New York: Livewright Publishing Company, 1935. 412 pp.

51. Freud, Sigmund. The Interpretation of Dreams. Authorized translation by James Strachey. New York: Basic Books, 1955. 692 pp.

52. Freud, Sigmund. Totem and Taboo. Authorized English translation by James Strachey. New York: W. W. Norton and Company, 1950.

53. Freud, Sigmund. Three Essays on the Theory of Sexuality. Authorized translation by James Strachey. London: Imago Publishing Company, 1949. 133 pp.

54. Gandía, Enrique de. Cultura y folklore en América. Buenos Aires: Editorial El Ateneo, 1947. 375 pp.

55. Glover, Edward. Freud or Jung. New York: W. W. Norton and Company, 1950.

56. Guerrero, Javier. "Consideraciones sobre folklore y ciencia folklórica." Caracas: Archivos Venezolanos de Folklore, Year I, no. 1., January–June 1951, pp. 43–103.

57. Hegel, Georg. Philosophy of Mind. Translated from the Encyclopedia of the Philosophical Sciences by William Wallace. Oxford: The Clarendon Press, 1894. 320 pp.

58. Herskovits, Melville J. Man and His Works: The Science of Cultural Anthropology. New York: A. A. Knopf, 1948. 678 pp.

59. Herzog, George. "Investigación sobre la música primitiva y folklorica en los Estados Unidos." Montevideo: Instituto Interamericano de Musicología. Boletín Latino-Americano de Música, 1941, Vol. V, first part, pp. 393–420.

60. Hoyos Sáinz, Luis and Hoyos Sancho, Nieves. Manual de folklore. Madrid: Manuales de la Revista de Occidente, 1947. 602 pp. with illustrations.

61. IBECC. 1º Congresso Brasileiro de Folclore (1951). Anais Vol. I, Rio de Janeiro: Ministério de Relações Exteriores, 1952. 142 pp.

62. Imbelloni, José. Concepto y praxis del folklore como ciencia. Buenos Aires: Editorial Humanior, 1943. 136 pp. with illustrations.

63. Imbelloni, José. "Un escándalo científico: las libretas íntimas de Lévy-Bruhl." Buenos Aires: *Runa*, Vol. III, part 1–2, 1950. pp. 217–221.
64. Jacovella, Bruno. *Manual-Guía para el recolector*. La Plata: Instituto de la Tradición, 1951. 48 pp.
65. Jijena Sánchez, Rafael. "El folklore. Sus métodos y sus conquistas." Buenos Aires: *Primer Ciclo Anual de Conferencias,* Subsecretaría de Cultura de la Nación, 1950, pp. 217–241.
66. Jijena Sánchez, Rafael. *Instrucciones generales para la recolección de material folklórico.* Tucumán: Universidad Nacional de Tucumán, Instituto de Historia, Lingüística y Folklore, 1942. 8 pp.
67. Jijena Sánchez, Rafael and Jacovella, Bruno. *Las supersticiones. Contribución a la metodología de la investigación folklórica.* Buenos Aires: Ediciones Buenos Aires, 1939. 154 pp.
68. Jover Peralta, Anselmo. *El guaraní en la geografía de América. Diccionario de guaranismos.* Buenos Aires: Editorial Tupa, 1950. 272 pp.
69. Kardiner, Abram. *The Individual and his Society; the Psychodynamics of Primitive Social Organization.* New York: Columbia University Press, 1939. 503 pp.
70. Laytano, Dante de. *História de uma palavra.* Rio de Janeiro: CNFL, Semana Folklórica, 1948, pp. 67–70.
71. Lévy-Bruhl, Lucien. *Primitive Mentality.* Authorized translation by Lilian A. Clare. London: George Allen and Unwin, Ltd. 1923. 458 pp.
72. Lévy-Bruhl, Lucien. *How Natives Think.* Authorized translation by Lilian A. Clare. New York: Alfred A. Knopf, Inc., 1966.
73. Lévy-Bruhl, Lucien. *Les carnets de Lucien Lévy-Bruhl.* Preface by Maurice Leenhardt. Library of Contemporary Philosophy founded by Félix Alcan. Paris: Presses Universitaires de France, 1949. 255 pp.
74. Lima, Raúl. "El falso folklore." Tucumán, *Boletín de la Asociación Tucamana de Folklore,* Year II, Vol. I, No. 19–20, 1951, pp. 199–200.
75. Lourenço Filho. *Curso de psicología educacional.* Rio de Janeiro: Faculdade Nacional de Filosofia, 1946–1947. Mimeographed class notes.
76. Lowie, Robert H. *The History of Ethnological Theory.* New York: Rinehart, 1939. 296 pp.
77. Malinowski, Bronislaw. *A Scientific Theory of Culture and Other Essays.* Chapel Hill: The University of North Carolina Press, 1944. 228 pp.
78. Marinus, Albert. *Critique, méthode et conceptions dans le folklore.* 3rd edition. Brussels: Service des reserches historiques et folkloriques du Brabant, 1935. 23 pp.
79. Marinus, Albert. *La causalité folklorique.* Brussels: Imprimerie Charles Peeters Léau, 1942. 92 pp.

80. Molinari, Hernando. "Sobre literatura infantil." Yaguarón, *Revista Ihsoindih,* Year I, no. 3., IIId era, pp. 1–3.

81. Molina-Téllez, Félix. *El mito, la leyenda y el hombre.* Buenos Aires: Editorial Claridad, 1947. 289 pp. with illustrations.

82. Morote Best, Efraín. *El Dr. Ralph Steele Boggs y su clasificación del folklore.* Cuzco: Universidad Nacional del Cuzco, 1954. 58 pp.

83. Morote Best, Efraín. *Elementos de folklore. Definición, contenido, procedimiento.* Cuzco: Universidad Nacional de Cuzco, 1950. 511 pp.

84. Moya, Ismael. *Didáctica del folklore.* Buenos Aires: Editorial El Ateneo, 1948. There is a 2nd edition corrected and augmented by Editorial Schapire S. R. L. Buenos Aires: 1956. 244 pp.

85. Navarro del Aguila, Víctor. "Perú: Instituto de Folklore y Lenguas Indígenas del Cuzco." México: *Boletín Indigenista,* Vol. XII, no. 4., 1952, pp. 320–330.

86. Nina Rodrigues, Raimundo. *O animismo fetichista dos negros bahianos.* Preface and notes by Arthur Ramos. Rio de Janeiro: Civilização Brasileira, S. A., 1935. 199 pp. The first French edition was published in 1900.

87. Núñez y Domínguez, José de J. "La importancia del folklore." Mexico: *Anales de la Sociedad Folklórica de México,* Vol. II, 1941, Mexico: 1942.

88. Ogden, C. K. and Richards, I. A. *The Meaning of Meaning.* New York: Harcourt, Brace and Company, 1946. 363 pp.

89. Ortega Ricaurte, Daniel. "Folklore indígena." Bogotá: *Revista de Folklore,* no. 6., January 1951. pp. 177–184.

90. Ortiz, Fernando. "Discurso." Vitória, Espírito Santo. Comissão Espirito-Santense de Folclore. *Folclore,* Year VI, No. 32–33.

91. Osmar Gomes, Antônio. "Estudos de folclore." Rio de Janeiro: *Jornal do Comércio,* August 29, 1940.

92. Pierson, Donald. *Teoria e pesquisa em Sociologia.* São Paulo: Edições Melhoramentos, 1948. 448 pp.

93. Poviña, Alfredo. *Curso de sociología.* 2nd edition. Vol. II. Córdoba: Editorial Assandri, 1950. 817 pp.

94. Radcliffe-Brown, A. R. "On the Concept of Function in Social Science." *American Anthropologist.* Vol. 37, July–September 1935, pp. 394–402.

95. Ramos, Arthur. *A aculturação negra no Brasil.* Rio de Janeiro: Companhia Editôra Nacional, 1942. 376 pp.

96. Ramos, Arthur. Conceito de folclore. Rio de Janeiro: *Semana Folclórica,* 1948, pp. 18–21.

97. Ramos, Arthur. "Cultura e ethnos." Rio de Janeiro: Ministério de Educação. *Cultura,* Year I, no. 1., 1948, pp. 87–96.

98. Ramos, Arthur. *Estudos de folk-lore.* Rio de Janeiro: Livraria Editôra da Casa do Estudante do Brasil, 1952. 191 pp.

99. Ramos, Arthur. *Freud, Adler, Jung. Ensáios de psicanálise ortodoxa*

e herética. Preface by Afrânio Peixoto. Rio de Janeiro: Editôra Guanabara, 1933. 240 pp.

100. Ramos, Arthur. *Introdução à antropologia brasileira.* Vol. I. Rio de Janeiro: Casa do Estudante do Brasil, 1943. 540 pp.

101. Ramos, Arthur. *Introducão à Psicologia Social.* Rio de Janeiro: Livraria José Olympio, Editôra, 1936. 371 pp.

102. Ramos, Arthur. *Loucura e crime. Questões de Psiquitria, Medicina Forense e Psicologia Social.* Preface by Josué de Castro. Porto Alegre: Livraria do Globo, 1937. 206 pp.

103. Ramos, Arthur. *O folk-lore negro do Brasil. Demopsicologia e psicanálise.* Rio de Janeiro: Editôra Civilização Brasileira, S. A., 1935. 279 pp.

104. Ramos, Arthur. *O negro brasileiro. Etnografia religiosa.* 2nd augmented edition. Rio de Janeiro: Cia. Editôra Nacional, 1940. 343 pp. The first edition was published in 1934.

105. Real Torralba, Félix. "El delicado problema de la literatura infantil." Yaguarón: *Ihsoindih,* Year I, no. 3., IIId era, pp. 1–3.

106. Ribeiro, Joaquim. *Folclore brasileiro.* Rio de Janeiro: Zélio Valverde, 1944. 222 pp.

107. Ribot, Théodule. *La lógica de los sentimientos.* Translated by Ricardo Rubio. Madrid: Daniel Jorro, 1905. 239 pp.

108. Rocha de Mello e Souza, Gilda. "A moda no século XIX. Ensaio de sociologia estética." Sao Paulo: *Revista do Museu Paulista,* new series, Vol. V., 1951, pp. 7–94.

109. Romero, Jesús C. "El folklore en México." Mexico: *Sociedad Mexicana de Geografia y Estadistica,* 1947, pp. 559–798.

110. Schmidt, Wilhelm. *Manuale di metodologia etnológica.* Milan: Societá Editrice Vita E Pensiero, 1949. 325 pp.

111. Sébillot, Paul. *La Bretagne enchantée.* Paris: J. Maison-neuve Libraire-Editeur, n.d. 284 pp.

112. Sokolov, Y. M. *Russian folklore.* Translated by Catherine Ruth Smith. New York: The Macmillan Company, 1950. 757 pp.

113. Spencer, Herbert. *The Principals of Sociology.* New York: D. Appleton and Company, 1883.

114. Sumner, William Graham. *Folkways.* New York: Athenaeum Press, 1906.

115. Tavares de Lima, Rossini. *ABC de folklore.* São Paulo: Publicação do Conservatório Dramático e Musical, 1952. 134 pp.

116. Thoms, W. J. "Folk-lore." Reprint of the letter by W. J. Thoms in *Athenaeum* of August 22, 1846. In Alan Dundes, *The Study of Folklore.* Englewood Cliffs, New Jersey: Prentice-Hall, 1965.

117. Tylor, Edward B. *Primitive Culture,* 2 vols. New York: Henry Holt and Company, 1874.

118. UNESCO. *Declaratoria sobre la raza.* México: Boletín Indigenista, Vol. X, No. 1., 1950, pp. 10–18.

119. Valbuena. *Novísimo diccionario español-latino.* Revised edition,

corrected and augmented by Miguel de Toro y Gómez. Paris: Garnier Brothers Publishers, 1923 (?) . 1,287 pp.

120. Van Gennep, Arnold. *La formación de las leyendas.* Spanish version by Guillermo Escobar. Madrid: Librería Gutenberg of José Cruz, 1914. 312 pp. (Library of Scientific Philosophy edited by Gustavo Le Bon.)

121. Van Gennep, Arnold. *Manuel de folklore français contemporain.* Vol. I. Paris: Éditions Auguste Picard, 1943. 375 pp.

122. Vega, Carlos. *Panorama de la música popular argentina. Con un ensayo sobre la ciencia del folklore.* Buenos Aires: Editorial Losada. S. A., 1944. 361 pp.

123. Vox. *Diccionario general ilustrado de la lengua española.* Prologue by Don Ramón Menéndez Pidal. 2nd corrected edition by D. Samuel Gili Gaya. Barcelona: Publicaciones y Ediciones SPES, S. A., 1953. 1,815 pp.

Index